N H Richardson

THE MINISTER IN THE REFORMED TRADITION

THE MINISTER IN THE REFORMED TRADITION

Harry G. Goodykoontz

JOHN KNOX PRESS
Richmond, Virginia

TO
MY WIFE, BETTY

Preface

Who and what is a minister? During the first few years of my ministry this question did not concern me, but for twenty years I have been giving it much thought. During the Second World War, some church members confused their concept of patriotism with religion. When a minister failed to justify the war effort in a manner pleasing to these members, they would insinuate that he was disloyal, and would try to undermine his place in the church. This happened to several ministers I knew. In the years since, I have been forced to think more deeply concerning the ordained ministry.

One of the great rediscoveries of our time is the place of the layman in the life of the church. The World Council of Churches has emphasized the fact that the church is not constituted of clergy alone but of clergy and laity. The Reformation doctrine of the priesthood of believers has come alive. This has led some to ask, why a special order of ministers?

During the five years that I served my denomination as its director of student work, I had some rewarding ecumenical experiences. I learned that the chief theological stumbling block to the unity of the church is the doctrine of the church, particularly the doctrine of the ministry. The problem of inter-communion, for instance, roots in the question, What is a valid ministry?

When I began to teach in a theological seminary, I soon learned that the chief problem of seminary students is one of identification. Who am I? This was first seen to be true on the psychological level, but in time I realized that many a seminary student does not know the meaning of the role of an ordained minister. A Baptist hospital chaplain who gives clinical training to students from half a dozen seminaries and as many denominations says that the first thing he has to teach these men is to enter the patient's room as a minister of the gospel, not just to make a social call. Indeed, many an ordained minister has no clear self-image as a minister.

7

The minister today, lacking a secure assurance of who he is, does not grasp the nature of his authority. In fact, he may even dodge the issue and evade some of his responsibility by placing all his stress on the ministry of the laity. The minister is confused. The people are confused. And no definitive word can be spoken on the subject at present. It is hoped that this book will speak an authentic word. I write from within the framework of the Reformed theology and the Presbyterian system, and what is said will be colored by that perspective, from which I view the nature of the minister and his authority. The basic question is common to all denominations: What *is* a minister of Word and Sacrament?

Of this I am certain: if the minister does not respect his role or understand his place in the church, no one else is likely to do so for long. If the minister does not know who he is, his people are likely to be confused also. My prayer is that this book may cast some light on the darkness.

* * *

The initial research on this volume was done while the author was on sabbatical leave, studying at New College, University of Edinburgh. My gratitude is herewith expressed to the Advanced Religious Study Foundation for making possible that study. The resources of the following libraries have been at my disposal: Louisville Presbyterian Seminary, New College, Princeton Theological Seminary, and the Presbyterian Historical Foundation at Montreat, N. C. The respective librarians and staff members were uniformly helpful. I am grateful to Drs. L. C. Rudolph and Albert C. Winn, who critically read the entire manuscript, and to other members of the Louisville Presbyterian Seminary faculty with whom I have talked over various ideas incorporated in this book. Members of the staff of John Knox Press have been of great assistance in helping me to reduce the manuscript to reasonable length, improve the style, and be accurate in my references. My family during the long months of typing and retyping, and checking of ancient references, were wonderfully patient (most of the time!).

H.G.G.

Contents

I

------·····◄◅◦▻····------

THE MINISTER TODAY

The church has today no common doctrine of the ministry. For this reason, many ministers and laymen are confused about the nature of the ordained ministry. The revival of the doctrine of the priesthood of believers has led some to question the validity of an order or even an office of the ministry. If every Christian is a minister, why should some Christians be ordained to special, lifelong privileges which the layman can never have? In this democratic era, is there any place for a spiritual aristocracy even of so mild a sort as the Protestant ministry? Are the theological debates over the validity of ministerial orders archaic nonsense, or do they grow out of something deeply meaningful? What authority does the minister possess? Does the Reformed concept of the ministry as developed by Calvin, Knox, and others in the sixteenth century, have a continuing relevance for modern man, or do we need an entirely new concept of the ministry for the space age? Does the Bible set forth concerning the ministry an irrevocable form or a basic principle with dynamic force and a growing edge?

At the operational level, is the minister to be a "steward of the mysteries of God" or is he to be a glorified business manager, subject to the board of directors who can fire him if he does not produce results satisfactory to them? Is he an "ambassador of Christ" or is he a "priest of the American way of life"? Is he to strive diligently for a larger membership roll, or for a deeper experience of Christ on the part of those already members? Such questions are neither silly nor simple. Sooner or later every minister faces some questions such as these.

Professor Samuel Blizzard in a valuable study[1] has shown us that the

11

American minister lives in a state of confusion and frustration because he has one concept of his role and his people have another. The minister thinks of himself as a preacher and pastor, but his people want him first of all to be an organizer and administrator. The recruiting leaflets for the ministry stress the ancient and glamorous roles of pastor and preacher, but the congregation wants a man who can keep the wheels moving. The minister finds himself spending most of his time doing the things which he enjoys the least. It frustrates a man to find himself spending more time typing and mimeographing than studying. Trained to proclaim the Word of God, the average minister now gives over half of his time to organization and administration. No wonder his self-image is blurred! Despite the contention that ministers break down because they work seventy hours a week and still can never complete their task, the role confusion and the blurred self-image involved therein are far more likely to cause ministerial breakdowns.

Traumatic, perhaps, is the shock that comes to a minister when he learns that his vocation, which had been presented to him as a noble calling, is looked upon with mild contempt by many. The ministry is "the third sex," more adept at tasting tea than at turning a lathe, more at home with the young mothers' circle than with a baseball team. So the word comes from the seat of the scornful. Who over age thirty can forget the screen ministers portrayed by a Caspar Milquetoast personality? Such characterizations are grossly unfair to the ministry, but there is just enough truth in them to hurt and to confuse.

What the people expect of the minister varies from community to community, but often it is at odds with the expectations of the minister himself. Although some expectations are culturally rooted, others have theological overtones. To some laymen, the minister is the man who eases their conscience. They have hired him to be religious for them. He is to pray at all meetings, and is to do all of the pastoral visiting and all of the evangelistic calling. Other laymen want the minister to preach and visit the sick, and to leave everything else to the laymen. They want him to keep hands off the Sunday school, the church finances, and the social life of the church. Where the ministry of the laity is rightly understood, however, these two extremes are avoided and the clergy-laity axis is well-balanced.

The Bible often creates gnawing uncertainty in the minister's mind. He knows that it is deeply relevant to every age, yet he may be basically unsure of himself as an interpreter of the Word of God. "Who am I that I should set myself up as an unfolder of the Word of God?" Why is my interpretation any better than that of many intelligent laymen in my congregation? Does my seminary training make any difference? Furthermore, the perennial conflict between the scholarly understanding of the Scriptures which the minister has and the naïve views held by many of his congregation may be a source of difficulty. How much shall my critical studies affect my sermons? Shall I prepare my young people for what they will hear in high school and college of the critical views of the Bible and indeed of the Christian faith? Many seminary students go through a period of uncertainty as they wrestle with biblical interpretations and theological problems on which good and learned men differ greatly in their conclusions. A large number go into their first pastorate with some of this uncertainty unresolved.

The minister's confusion is compounded by that of his people. In any congregation there are likely to be some who idolize the minister —any minister—and some who tolerate him. Some look upon the preacher as a veritable messenger of God, and will take from his lips words they would not permit any other person to speak. Others constantly fume because, "The minister, who is no better than I am, tries to tell me how to live." Some frankly expect the minister and his family to live on a higher plane than do the other families of the congregation. Other folk believe that there ought to be no difference between the conduct of the minister's family and the conduct of the other families of the church. Some believe that the minister, though an earthen vessel, is used mightily of God, while others spend all their time commenting on the earthenness of the vessel. Some believe that the pastor ought to call in every home regularly, others prefer to be left alone.

Heated confusion gathers around the question of the freedom of the pulpit. Some people want the minister to "preach the Bible," while others want him to "be relevant to the needs of modern man." These two desires are not necessarily contradictory, but they do not automatically merge as some naïvely think. What has the gospel of forgiveness to do with foreign aid or the problem of integration? What has faith to do with juvenile delinquency? One says, "When I go to church I want to hear something spiritual, not something I can hear at my civic club." Another says, "Our preacher is so old-fashioned he just preaches the Bible, and it is so boring." Multiplied comments along these lines add to the confusion of both laity and clergy. Is the pulpit free, so the minister can preach prophetic as well as pastoral sermons? Or should the minister be muzzled when it comes to the implications of the gospel for such matters as race, economics, international relations, and politics?

In recent years a number of ministers have lost their pulpits because of their efforts to have their people adopt Christian attitudes toward the question of integration. Granted that some ministers have been unwise, and have made of race relations an obsession, it is still true that some men have been dismissed from their churches because they tried honestly to proclaim the meaning of the gospel for this area of life. In a Presbyterian church, in which the pulpit is solely the responsibility of the minister, who is subject not to the congregation or the official board but to the presbytery, the matter may not come out into the open. On occasion, a specious charge has been framed and the matter taken to presbytery, but everyone has recognized that the real trouble grew out of the minister's "liberal views on the race question." Such instances are rare; more frequently a man "secures a call to a larger field" (under pressure). Some men, secure because their people love them, have been fearless in their proclamation of the implications of the gospel for relations between the races. For a century, however, there has been more soft-pedaling on this issue than one likes to admit. There are places where ministers have been told by their people to keep their mouths shut concerning integration. Neither courage nor lack of it is limited to ministers in any particular size of church or type of congregation—or denomination. In some sections of the country the crucial issue is not race but economics. The middle-class culture of the Protestant churches significantly tones down the prophetic message of many a pulpit.

Some laymen bitterly resent the practical implications which their ministers have drawn from the gospel. The time-honored concept of the minister as prophet is at stake. Some years ago at a meeting of a high church court an emotionally excited layman in the heat of debate charged that the ministers of the church were trying to lead it down the garden path to socialism, and called upon the elders to arise and save the church from its ministers. This attitude that the ministers of the church are not to be trusted because of their "social radicalism," their "internationalism," or their "theological liberalism," is held by too many laymen. Not by the most able, not by the most wise, but by too many, some of whom ought to know better. A vicious effort, not limited to any one denomination, is being made to bring about a cleavage between the clergy and laity. Part of the difficulty stems from the fact that many godly laymen are theologically untrained and simply do not realize that a profound biblical-theological understanding lies beneath certain views to which ministers tend to adhere, e.g., support of the United Nations. Further, ministers motivated by deep compassion for the underprivileged and the needy and the oppressed may sometimes venture into phases of social reform that more timid folk will eschew.

Privileged groups tend to fight fiercely against anything that will hurt their pocketbooks. Some of these have been behind the moves to create a split between the clergy and the laity. Some good but rather thoughtless people believe misrepresentations and charges often based on quotations taken out of context. Many laymen, devout but misguided, are inclined to be suspicious of their ministers. This suspicion occasionally may be grounded in theology, and often pretends to be, but it is usually geared in to an economic or sociological point of view. A vast majority of the laity, fortunately, support the clergy, and most laymen deplore all efforts to create a split. Tensions are inevitable in any organization, even in the church. Recent studies of power structures and authority figures in the life of the church witness to the reality of tensions.[2] Often tensions develop and intensify between immature persons. Immaturity is closely related to a fuzzy self-image. If the minister is badly confused as to his role, he is likely to be unsure and inefficient in his relations with others. Two psychologists have shown that there is an inseparable relationship between identity and interpersonal competence.[3]

In this chapter we have endeavored to highlight a few of the reasons why many ministers today are somewhat unsure of themselves as ministers. Lest the picture seem too dark, let us add that most ministers have a fairly good idea of who they are, and most ministers are happy in their vocation. Most laymen sincerely respect their minister, even though they may misunderstand his role.

II

---◦◦◦◦◦---

THE BIBLICAL VIEW OF
THE MINISTRY

A major reason for the minister's fuzzy self-image is that there is no clear statement in the Bible concerning the nature of the ministry. The Bible says many things about the ministry, but nothing definitive. Able scholars differ in their interpretations. Is the ministry primarily an office or a function, or is it both? Are bishops of the *esse*, or of the *bene esse*, or simply of the fullness of the church? In fact, are they even desirable? Is apostolic succession plain nonsense or does the concept contain basic truth? Such questions arouse strong emotions. Pure objectivity is impossible. The biblical scholar who thinks he is objective is certain to be influenced more than he realizes by his own denominational background, by the age in which he lives, and by his own psychological conditioning. In this, the scholar is not being dishonest, he is simply being human.

In recent discussions of the biblical view of the ministry, agreement has been reached on several points. (1) Ministry means service. (2) The one essential ministry is that of Jesus Christ, which he carries out through his church. (3) The whole church engages in this ministry. (4) Some are set apart for a special ministry. (5) This ministry has various forms, but there is only one ministry.

THE FUNDAMENTAL CONCEPT—SERVANTHOOD

The New Testament concept of the ministry has certain roots in the Old Testament, where prophets, priests, and even kings were called of God to be his ministers. It is along the line of the Suffering Servant, portrayed in the magnificent fifty-third chapter of Isaiah, rather than along the line of the Levitical priesthood, that we find

17

the New Testament making its chief development. Jesus Christ, who "came not to be ministered unto, but to minister" (Matt. 20:28, KJV), embodies in his own life and work the description of the Suffering Servant. The Word of God incarnate had the form of a servant. "The whole office of the ministry is to be understood as the expression in the Church of this fundamental paradox—that Jesus Christ, the Son of God, the King of all the earth, comes and establishes His kingly rule among men in the form, not of a king, but of a servant."[1] One cannot read the Gospels without being aware of this marvelous truth. Each of the Gospels has a record of an incident, with an accompanying teaching, wherein it is made clear that Jesus is the Servant. Two of these passages concern the Last Supper, which sets forth the supreme symbol of the Suffering Servant—the lamb slain from before the foundation of the world. The Gospel of John records the story of Jesus washing the feet of his disciples. The story is set in the context of the upper room, with this significant introduction: ". . . when Jesus knew that his hour had come to depart out of this world to the Father, having loved his own who were in the world, he loved them to the end. . . . Jesus, knowing that the Father had given all things into his hands, and that he had come from God and was going to God, rose from supper, laid aside his garments, and girded himself with a towel. . . ." (John 13:1, 3-4). Having washed their feet, he said: "For I have given you an example, that you also should do as I have done to you" (John 13:15). Commenting on this, Bishop Westcott said, "The knowledge that He was possessed of this divine authority was the ground of His act of service."[2]

Luke 22:14-34, a passage also set in the upper room, shows the disciples, spiritually blind, disputing among themselves about which was the greatest. Jesus said, ". . . let the greatest among you become as the youngest, and the leader as one who serves. . . . But I am among you as one who serves" (Luke 22:26-27). The last sentence has been called the key to Jesus' ministry, and therefore the key to all Christian ministry.

Kindred teachings are found in Matthew 20:26-28 and Mark 10:42-45. The word translated "to serve" is from the Greek *diakoneo*, which literally means "to wait on tables, to function as a servant." The minister is one who serves. In Jesus we see the nature of the gospel ministry. "The prototype for the ministry is our Lord Himself; the pattern for all the New Testament has to say about the ministry is what our Lord has to say about His ministry."[3]

Jesus was a servant. He went about doing good. He ministered to the least, the lowest, and the lost. He helped rich and poor, young and old, Jew and Samaritan. And in the end, as the Holy Communion reminds us, he offered up himself "a full, perfect, and sufficient sacrifice," to reconcile us to God.

In passages of great beauty and tremendous theological significance, Paul and Peter hymn the servanthood of Jesus.

"Have this mind among yourselves, which you have in Christ Jesus, who, though he was in the form of God, did not count equality with God a thing to be grasped, but emptied himself, taking the form of a servant, being born in the likeness of men. And being found in human form he humbled himself and became obedient unto death, even death on a cross" (Phil. 2:5-8).

". . . because Christ also suffered for you, leaving you an example, that you should follow in his steps. . . . He himself bore our sins in his body on the tree, that we might die to sin and live to righteousness. By his wounds you have been healed. For you were straying like sheep, but have now returned to the Shepherd and Guardian of your souls" (1 Peter 2:21-25; see also 2 Cor. 8:9 and Heb. 5:8).

The book of Acts reveals that the disciples soon realized that to follow Jesus is to be a servant. Arrested, beaten, stoned, hounded from place to place, they learned in their own experience what it meant to take up their cross and follow him. They learned to bear in their own bodies the marks of the Lord Jesus. The Christian is to pour out his life in service as a sacrifice of praise. To be a minister is to be a servant.

THE CONTINUING MINISTRY OF JESUS CHRIST

There is but one essential ministry, that of Jesus Christ, the risen, ever-present Lord.[4] He who in Galilee and in Judea was carrying out the Messianic ministry of the Suffering Servant continues that ministry in and through his church, which is his body. As the body of which Christ is the Head, the church is manifestly more than just another human institution, more than a great organization. Despite its frailty and sinfulness, the church is the body of Christ, and in and through it Christ is carrying on his mission to the world. Paul in his letter to the Ephesians exhausts the resources of human language in describing the relationship of the church to its Lord. The church is the temple of which Christ is the chief cornerstone, she is the bride of Christ, purified by his matchless love for her.[5] The Johannine metaphor of the vine and the branches is of similar import. The biblical images of the church convey the ultimate fact that in some deep sense Jesus Christ is in and through and with his church, doing his work in the world. In the Christological passage Colossians 1:15-24, Jesus Christ is clothed with the attributes of deity. Christ is the head of the body, the church; and Paul, as a minister of that church, rejoices that in his sufferings he completes "what is lacking in Christ's afflictions for the sake of his body, that is, the church." Paul does not mean that Christ's sufferings and death were not adequate or final in significance, but he does mean that in some sense the disciples of Christ, doing his work, share his sufferings. Christ continues to minister to the world through the church, "which is his body, the fulness of him who fills all in all" (Eph. 1:23).

In First Corinthians 12 and in Romans 12, as well as in Ephesians and Colossians, Paul speaks of the church as the body, a living organism, a unity. In this body, "If one member suffers, all suffer together; if one member is honored, all rejoice together" (1 Cor. 12:26). The aim of the church in this functional unity is that man may find God in Christ and be redeemed. Jesus' prayer in the upper room for his disciples was ". . . that they may all be one; even as thou, Father, art in me, and I in thee, that they also may be in us, so that the world may believe that thou hast sent me" (John 17:21). Unity is essential for evangelization. In principle, the body of Christ has this unity; and it therefore has a mission to the world for the reconciliation of sinful mankind to the Father in heaven. The great commission in Matthew 28:18-20 states the purpose of the church: "Go . . . make disciples of all nations" (verse 19). The mission of the church is to preach, to teach, to baptize, always depending upon Christ's promise, "and lo, I am with you always, to the close of the age" (verse 20).

The risen, ascended Lord is in his church, carrying out his eternal purposes. The minister may be proud of his gospel (Rom. 1:16-17), yet he knows that he is but an earthen vessel (2 Cor. 4:7). Indeed, "For what we preach is not ourselves, but Jesus Christ as Lord, with ourselves as your servants for Jesus' sake" (2 Cor. 4:5). "We beseech you on behalf of Christ, be reconciled to God" (2 Cor. 5:20).

When we witness by word or by life, it is Jesus Christ who is with us to make our ministry dynamic and real. If it be not of Christ, it is not enough. His is the ministry! Our human ministries are "derivative, dependent, and functional."[6]

THE WHOLE CHURCH ENGAGES IN THIS MINISTRY

The great Reformation doctrine of the priesthood of believers is an effort to state the truth that Christ continues to minister through the whole church. His saving deed was done once for all; his atoning work does not need to be repeated; and certainly the church is not co-savior with its Lord. But he who was the great High Priest to end all priesthoods is also carrying out a priestly ministry through his body. The whole church has a priesthood to exercise, a ministry to perform, a gospel to proclaim. All Christians, minister and so-called laymen alike, constitute the people (*laos*, laity) of God. Every Christian therefore is in a sense a priest, a minister, a pastor, an evangelist.

The biblical term for the followers of Jesus is "disciples." "And the twelve summoned the body of the disciples and said . . ." (Acts 6:2a, 7; see John 8:31; Luke 9:1). These disciples partook of the ministry of the church. They were members of the royal priesthood that is the church. The references in the New Testament to the priesthood of believers are to the corporate body, the church. In the singular, priest is applied to Jesus only, not to the believer.[7] The church has a ministry, to reconcile the world to God in Christ. The church has a priesthood, ". . . and like living stones be yourselves built into a spiritual house, to be a holy priesthood, to offer spiritual sacrifices acceptable to God through Jesus Christ. . . . But you are a chosen race, a royal priesthood, a holy nation, God's own people, that you may declare the wonderful deeds of him who called you out of darkness into his marvelous light" (1 Peter 2:5, 9; see also Rev. 1:6 and 20:6).

The church is indeed a holy priesthood called to bear witness to God's redeeming grace in his Son. All Christians participate in this priesthood, just as all Christians partake of the one ministry. It is unfortunate that the biblical sense of a corporate priesthood degenerated into the excessive individualism that has plagued Protestantism. While the individual Christian does share in the priesthood, he also needs to participate in corporate worship and to pay heed to the teaching of the man in the pulpit. All Christians are disciples, learners of Christ. Each disciple, within the limits of the capacities God has given him, is to exercise his ministry where God has placed him. Some disciples are called to be pastors—ministers of Word and Sacrament.

SOME ARE SET APART FOR A SPECIAL MINISTRY

While it is true that the whole church engages in the ministry of Christ, it is also true that some men and women are called and set apart for a special ministry, that of Word and Sacrament. These constitute the ordained ministers of the church. The concept of ordination is discussed in chapter eight.

Our human ministries in and through the church are derived from the commission of Christ. A most important passage for the understanding of the ministry is Ephesians 4:7-16. Particularly significant are these words:

"But grace was given to each of us according to the measure of Christ's gift. . . . And his gifts were that some should be apostles, some prophets, some evangelists, some pastors and teachers, for the equipment of the saints, for the work of ministry, for building up the body of Christ . . ." (Eph. 4:7, 11-12).

It should be noted that most modern versions omit the comma after saints. The omitted comma signifies that the church officers are given to the church "for the equipment of the saints for the work of ministry . . ."

This passage strongly suggests that Christ gave to the church not only ministry in general but also specific men and women with the gifts needed to carry out specific forms of ministry. "Pastors and teachers" are surely the early ancestors of our ordained ministers. The men specially called and set apart—the ordained ministry—constitute a gift of the risen and ascended Lord to his church. The ordained ministry has several forms, but it is one ministry, a continuation of Christ's ministry. Christ has given three great gifts to the church—the Word, the sacraments, and the ministry.[8] All three are necessary to the well-being of the church. The Word cannot be adequately proclaimed without a ministry, and the sacraments cannot be orderly administered without a ministry or apart from the Word.

Not only is the ministry a gift to the church, it is also a gift of God to those whom he calls to be ministers. "You did not choose me, but I chose you and appointed you that you should go and bear fruit and that your fruit should abide . . ." (John 15:16). Jesus' words refer specifically to the eleven apostles, but indirectly to all disciples, including, surely, all ordained ministers. Paul contended that his apostleship was "not from men nor through man, but through Jesus Christ and God the Father . . ." (Gal. 1:1). Paul also spoke of "the stewardship of God's grace that was given to me for you" (Eph. 3:2; see also Eph. 3:7; 1 Cor. 1:1). Those whom God has set in the church to be its ministers have indeed a secret inner call from God. Their ministry, like that of the whole church, is derived from, is patterned after, and is dependent upon Jesus Christ. He who said I AM is eternally and dynamically present with his people as they carry out his commission (Matt. 28:20; John 15:5).

We have interpreted this Ephesians passage as indicating that God intended for his church to have an ordained ministry; some authorities do not think so. That the Bible described ministerial functions, tasks to be carried out by persons with proper gifts, is acknowledged by everyone. Most scholars of past generations, including Calvin, and most scholars of Catholic schools of thought today, see evidence of ministerial office as well as function in the New Testament. Many scholars of late have been stressing the functional aspect and questioning the office. It seems to modern scholars that it is unlikely that the churches of Paul's time had reached the point of having a regular organization with officers. It is usually taken for granted today that the lists of ministries in the New Testament church were originally lists of functions which became offices if they continued.

This assumption is without proof, and it is possible that the older scholars were correct in interpreting some of these words as referring to offices. Seemingly unimportant, actually such matters as apostolic succession and the validity of ministerial orders ride upon this question of office or function. J. K. S. Reid in his excellent monograph, *The Biblical Doctrine of the Ministry*, carefully examines the question and comes to the conclusion that in the Bible, ministry partakes both of office and of function.[9] Although it is clear that some persons were called to carry out ministerial functions, there are strong hints in the later books of the New Testament that some people were called to ministerial offices. We shall examine the main biblical words and passages to gain a clearer perspective on this matter.

ONE MINISTRY IN MANY FORMS

The one ministry is that of Jesus Christ, carried out in and through his church. He gave the church leaders, capable of carrying out specific tasks of service. As time passed, the necessity of organization led to the setting apart of some to special offices within the church. In the general sense, all of these are ministers. The function of the ministry is to equip the saints "for the work of ministry, for building up the body of Christ." Two terms in particular need to be examined before we look at the classic lists of ministerial functions (or offices).

The Twelve. The choice of twelve apostles was deliberate, a symbolical parallel with the twelve sons of Jacob. Jesus as the Messiah became also the Remnant, the living embodiment of the people of God, the new Israel which is the church. "The choice of twelve means that the new Israel, the Israel which has received the Messiah, is making a fresh start from the twelve apostles, as the old Israel started its history from the twelve sons of Jacob."[10] An eschatological place is given to the twelve. ". . . when the Son of man shall sit on his glorious throne, you who have followed me will also sit on twelve thrones, judging the twelve tribes of Israel" (Matt. 19:28; compare Rev. 20:4). The story of the election of an apostle to replace Judas shows that the twelve was an office and not simply a function. The twelve was a temporary but also a necessary office, not continued beyond the death of those who followed Jesus during all his ministry and were witnesses of the Resurrection (Acts 1:21-26). When James died, he was not replaced.

The Apostles (from the Greek, *apostello*, to send). An apostle is a messenger, one sent on a mission, with specific orders and delegated authority. The title "apostle" was usually restricted to the Twelve, along with Paul. The usage was a bit fluid, however, for Barnabas (Acts 14:14), James, the Lord's brother (Gal. 1:19), and several others were also called apostle. In the wider usage the term "apostle" is roughly synonymous with missionary. An apostle is one commissioned by the risen Christ to be "entrusted with the gospel" (Gal. 2:7).

The apostle is an ambassador sent on a mission. The word has the overtones of the Hebrew *shaliach*, a designated agent, an ambassador clothed with the authority of the sender. "A man's *shaliach* [agent] is as it were himself," the rabbis put it. Jesus said, "He who receives you receives me, and he who receives me receives him who sent me" (Matt. 10:40). The high church Anglican party has made a great deal of this concept of the power of the *shaliach*, the apostle.[11] T. W. Manson with brilliant scholarship has shown that the *shaliach* did not have the power to pass on his authority to others.[12] Only the king or master who sent the *shaliach* could pass on such authority to another. This is a powerful argument against the theory of apostolic succession. Nevertheless, overtones of office accrue to this powerful functional word, apostle.

The office of apostle no longer exists. The church itself is apostolic in nature, sent by God to witness to the world. All Christians, including ordained ministers, are sent by Christ into the world to proclaim the gospel. Writing from an Anglo-Catholic point of view, Alan Richardson says, "What we have in the Lucan story of the Last Supper is nothing less than an account of the ordination of the apostolic ministry of the Church in a eucharistic setting . . ." He goes on to say that the words of Jesus there ". . . constitute the rite of the ordination of the royal priesthood of the New Israel."[13] This apostolic ministry partakes of oversight (*episcope*), priesthood (*hierosune*), and service (*diakonia*). The continuing ministry in the church will always be with these notes, though ordination will no longer be "by the direct, unmediated action of the Risen Lord . . . but by his action through his body, the Church . . ."[14] Richardson, despite some dubious Anglo-Catholic implications which follow, is on the right track. So good a Protestant as John Calvin believed that knowledge concerning the work of the ministry could be derived from a study of the work of the apostles, especially Paul.[15] Such a study revealed the following ideas that are relevant to the ordained ministry as well as to the apostles.

(1) The apostles were men called, chosen, appointed (Matt. 10:1-4; Acts 1:2; 1 Tim. 1:12; 2:7, etc.).

(2) The apostles were eyewitnesses (Acts 1:21-22). The book of Acts reveals that "with great power the apostles gave their testimony to the resurrection of the Lord Jesus" (Acts 4:33a; see also Acts 5:32, 40, and especially 1 John 1:1: "That which was from the beginning, which we have heard, which we have seen with our eyes, which we have looked upon and touched with our hands, concerning the word of life . . ."). The apostles, called to be eyewitnesses, found their sufficiency not in their own wisdom but in God (2 Cor. 3:5-6).

(3) The apostleship is an office or perhaps a function of ministry, not one of self-glory (Acts 1:17-25; see Peter's exhortation to humility, 1 Peter 5:1-5).

(4) The apostles preached the Word authentically. When Jesus sent out the Twelve, they were charged, "And preach as you go, saying, 'The kingdom of heaven is at hand'" (Matt. 10:7). Preaching and teaching were part of the Great Commission (Matt. 28:18-20). Preaching, taken in the larger sense to include teaching and manner of life, was always at the core of the work. The apostles proclaimed the Word of God, and they believed themselves to have a message from their Lord to the world. Paul's words to Thessalonica are typical: "And we also thank God constantly for this, that when you received the word of God which you heard from us, you accepted it not as the word of men but as what it really is, the word of God, which is at work in you believers" (1 Thess. 2:13; compare Gal. 1:8, 11-12). Paul had deep certainty that his gospel was in line with the whole apostolic tradition, that he proclaimed the very word of God. "For I received from the Lord what I also delivered to you, that the Lord Jesus on the night when he was betrayed took bread . . ." (1 Cor. 11:23; see also 14:37; 15:3-8). Peter, too, was convinced that he preached God's word (1 Peter 1:12).

(5) The apostles exercised real authority, though tenderly. They

must have carried on their work much as do missionaries today in regions where the gospel is being first proclaimed, before an indigenous church has come into being. They emulated the Master in that they spoke with authority. They pronounced judgments (1 Cor. 5:3-5; 2 Cor. 13:2; 1 Thess. 4:10-12, 15). Paul was sometimes certain that he was saying exactly what God wanted him to say, and sometimes felt he must add, "I say, not the Lord" (1 Cor. 7:12). The parallel between Paul and the modern minister is manifest. The spirit which Paul had as he exercised authority is revealed in the Corinthian correspondence (2 Cor. 12:19). The apostles also gave orders (2 Tim. 3:14-15 and 4:11-15). Further, they expected obedience, though this obedience was ultimately not to themselves but to the Lord. "So then, brethren, stand firm and hold to the traditions which you were taught by us, either by word of mouth or by letter" (2 Thess. 2:15).[16]

The authority which the apostles exercised was always in the spirit of tenderness, much as good parents exercise a gentle firmness with their children. The apostles exercised more authority than would a minister today, for they were in a missionary situation, in an authoritarian environment, whereas our ministers are not in a missionary situation in the same sense, and are in a democratic age.

Paul in a wonderfully gentle way acted as a father to his children (Rom. 1:11-12; 9:3; 10:1). Two samples of his attitude reveal much. "I do not write this to make you ashamed, but to admonish you as my beloved children. For though you have countless guides in Christ, you do not have many fathers. For I became your father in Christ Jesus through the gospel. I urge you, then, be imitators of me" (1 Cor. 4:14-16). "For I wrote you out of much affliction and anguish of heart and with many tears, not to cause you pain but to let you know the abundant love that I have for you" (2 Cor. 2:4; compare 2 Cor. 10:1, 8-10; 3:2-3; 11:22-29). To Timothy, Paul wrote: "And the Lord's servant must not be quarrelsome but kindly to every one, an apt teacher, forbearing, correcting his opponents with gentleness" (2 Tim. 2:24-25). This ministry of authority was not one of prideful domination, nor of harsh authoritarianism, but of love. This apostle would never have been found exuding hostility, pounding the pulpit, berating his people for their wickedness. His rebukes were stern but loving.

(6) The apostles were not authoritarian dictators. They held a

most significant office in a manner worthy of the gospel, and therefore they were respected, loved, and heeded. But on basic issues they did not make the decisions for the church. Acts 15 contains the account of the first great church conference. When the Jewish Christians, who believed that salvation included being circumcised according to the Mosaic law, came to Antioch and taught thus, Paul and Barnabas strongly opposed them. The church at Antioch appointed Paul and Barnabas and others to go up to Jerusalem "to the apostles and the elders about this question" (Acts 15:2). Peter agreed with Paul and Barnabas. James the Lord's brother gave his judgment, which was a summary of the convictions that the assembly had reached, not a dogmatic utterance which the gathering had to swallow. Paul and Barnabas as well as Peter and James were influential in the discussion, but in the end it was the decision of the whole group. "For it has seemed good to the Holy Spirit and to us . . ." (vs. 28). From the beginning, when major decisions had to be made, the church in congregational meeting, or more likely the church through its chosen representatives, made the decisions. No one apostle, not even all of the apostles together, but the apostles along with the elders made the decision at the Jerusalem assembly.

(7) The apostles were always servants of God first, then servants of the people. James, Jude, Peter, and Paul all called themselves servants of Jesus Christ (James 1:1; Jude 1:1; 2 Peter 1:1; and Phil. 1:1). "Therefore, knowing the fear of the Lord, we persuade men" (2 Cor. 5:11a). Never is it the other way around. "Fearing God, we fear no man," was the attitude of Paul and the other apostles. Primarily a slave of Jesus, the apostle also serves his fellow men. "Even if I am to be poured as a libation upon the sacrificial offering of your faith, I am glad and rejoice with you all" (Phil. 2:17). This self-giving love is reminiscent of the ministry of Jesus.

(8) The apostles had special powers. Probably these privileges and responsibilities apply to the apostles in the narrow sense only, not to ministers in general. The apostles, for instance, performed miracles. ". . . and many wonders and signs were done through the apostles" (Acts 2:43; see also 5:12, 16; 14:8-10; 19:11-12). Endowed with the Holy Spirit, the apostles performed these and other miracles. Few if any ministers today expect to perform miracles. Yet, there is no inherent reason why the Holy Spirit cannot work miracles through

modern Christians who trust him. The church was commissioned to heal.

THE LIST OF MINISTRIES

"All ministries are functions exercised by the Body of Christ through organs which are organs of the Body. Consequently it is the Church that is apostolic, and the apostle is an organ of the Church."[17]

The New Testament has several passages which contain lists of ministries performed by Christians. The lists refer either to offices (titles) or functions (tasks), or more likely to the two in a unity that cannot be divided. As indicated earlier, modern scholars tend to assume that it is unlikely that the churches of Paul's time had reached the point of having a regular organization with officers. But it is possible that the older scholars were correct in interpreting some of these words as referring to definite offices.

COMPARISON OF PASSAGES

Romans 12:6-8	*1 Corinthians 12:8-10*	*1 Corinthians 12:28*
prophecy	wisdom	apostles
serving	knowledge	prophets
teaching	faith	teachers
exhortation	gifts of healing	workers of miracles
contributors	miracles	healers
aid-givers	prophecy	helpers
acts of mercy	distinguishing between spirits	administrators
	tongues	tongues
	interpretation of tongues	(interpreters, vs. 30)

Acts 13:1	*1 Peter 4:11*	*Ephesians 4:7, 11-12*
prophets	utters oracles of God	apostles
teachers	renders service	prophets
(apostles)		evangelists
		pastors and teachers

The passages in Peter and in Romans deal with functions, as is true of the first list in Corinthians. The second list in Corinthians (1 Cor. 12:28) is probably functional but it takes on overtones of office.

The brief list in Acts hints at offices, while the passage in Ephesians is probably closer to office than to function. An office is meaningless without function, and the functional aspect is in Ephesians too. While the Pastoral Epistles do not contain such lists, they clearly delineate the requisites for the offices of deacon (1 Tim. 3:8-13) and bishop (1 Tim. 3:1-7). These offices will be discussed in chapter three.

1 Peter 4:1-11. Peter, writing to the churches of Asia Minor in A.D. 63 or 64, endeavors to encourage them. In this section, he is saying that the end is near, and is writing of the way Christians should live in the interim. "As each has received a gift, employ it for one another, as good stewards of God's varied grace." The various gifts of God are to be used for the mutual good of the brethren. Both preaching and practical service are given that God may be glorified.

Acts 13:1. "Now in the church at Antioch there were prophets and teachers . . . and Saul." Possibly by the time Luke wrote the Acts the words prophet and teacher had official connotations. Saul (Paul) and Barnabas are set apart by the Holy Spirit through the church for the work of apostleship.

Romans 12:4-8. Modern interpreters generally call this list functional, but Calvin in interpreting the passage spoke of offices. A word which causes much difficulty is *proistamenos*, unfortunately translated in the Revised Standard Version as "gives aid." The King James translation, "he that ruleth," with the connotation of administration, is far more accurate.[18] Both here and in the lists in Corinthians we are given the profoundly simple and dynamic principles that each gift is of God and that each gift is to be used not for our own enjoyment and advancement but that we may serve.[19] Luther said long ago that all gifts are from God, and since no one has all the gifts, each Christian should be humble!

1 Corinthians 12. Chapters 12 through 14 constitute a unit. The key passage for our purposes is 12:28, but the whole context is meaningful. It is the same Triune Deity—Spirit, Lord, God—who is the inspirer in every one of various gifts and varieties of service (12:4-6). The Spirit is manifested to each "for the common good" (12:7). Spiritual gifts and graces are not given us for our self-gratification, but for the good of the whole body. John Calvin comments: "Here . . . he orders every one to bring what he has to the common heap, and not keep back the gifts of God in the way of enjoying every one his own, apart from the others, but aim unitedly at the edification of all in common."[20] The gifts listed in 12:8-10 are capacities to perform tasks, not official positions.

A body has many members, whether we think of a human body or of the church, the body of Christ. No part may look upon itself with pride or look down upon any other part, for each part needs all the other parts, and each part has some contribution to make to the whole. "If one member suffers, all suffer together; if one member is honored, all rejoice together" (vs. 26). Calvin comments: ". . . no one has so much as to have enough within himself, so as not to require help from others."[21] This whole passage reminds us that every member has his function in the whole. There are no useless members in the church! The church of Christ at Corinth is called the body of Christ and each member is told that he individually is a member of that body (vs. 27). It is with this background that we look at 12:28, which Clarence Craig said may be "our earliest description of the Christian ministry."[22] The main thrust of chapters 12 through 14 is of functional Christian living. Calvin, however, made quite a point of the fact that the first part of the twelfth chapter emphasizes gifts, and the final part offices. Before an office is to be discharged, gifts must be received. "For the Lord did not appoint ministers, without first endowing them with the requisite gifts, and qualifying them for discharging their duty."[23]

"And God has appointed in the church first apostles, second prophets, third teachers, then workers of miracles, then healers, helpers, administrators, speakers in various kinds of tongues" (1 Cor. 12:28).

The offices are probably listed in order of dignity,[24] but the list does not set forth hierarchy. Craig thinks the order is both important and deliberate.[25] God has appointed (*etheto* is a strong word, here meaning set by virtue of the sovereign power of God) in the church these offices:

Apostles (see discussion earlier in this chapter).

Prophets—proclaimers of the divine revelation, men who interpret and apply the Scriptures wisely for current use. Possibly "prophet" is a synonym for preacher, but it is more likely that the Holy Spirit spoke through these men a divine revelation. By about A.D. 125 or earlier, the prophets constituted a distinct group who received messages by divine revelation.

Teachers. Calvin thought that the word is used here in the sense of pastor, with the connotation that the pastor maintains and promotes sound Christian teaching (doctrine).

Social workers. Thus Clarence Craig discerningly lumps three functions—workers of miracles, healers, and helpers.[26] Craig is right at least on his main point: practical service accompanies the preaching of the gospel. Helpers might have been deacons.

Administrators ("governments" in KJV). These are the elders, in charge of church discipline, men of gravity, experience, and wisdom. It seems probable that administrative work is deliberately subordinated to the teaching and preaching functions of the church.

Speakers in various kinds of tongues—overwhelming religious emotion expressed in ecstatic utterances. The church was embarrassed then, as now, by this gift (1 Cor. 12:1-4 and ch. 14). Verse 30 adds *interpreters of tongues.*

Not all possess the enumerated gifts (offices or functions), but there is a more excellent way which all Christians can possess, the way of love (1 Cor. 13).

Ephesians 4:7, 11-12. "But grace was given to each of us according to the measure of Christ's gift. . . . And his gifts were that some should be apostles, some prophets, some evangelists, some pastors and teachers, for the equipment of the saints, for the work of ministry, for building up the body of Christ . . ." This is the classic passage on the ministry in the New Testament. Neither Romans nor First Corinthians depicts a set of church offices. This passage, however, almost certainly names offices. The main point is that one of the great gifts of the ascended Christ to his church is the gift of ministry, and of specific persons carrying out definite functions of ministry with manifest connotations of ministerial office. F. W. Beare says that this passage was written with the twelfth chapter of First Corinthians in mind, and that the changes made involve a transformation in the concept of the ministry from function to office.[27] We should not expect to find a formal delineation of church orders this early in the history of the church, though the book of Acts reminds us that the church at Ephesus had elders or bishops.

Apostles and prophets are by most scholars considered to be temporary offices given by God that the church might be established. The mystery of Christ has now been revealed "to his holy apostles and prophets by the Spirit" (Eph. 3:4-5). In Ephesians 2:20 the household of God is said to be "built upon the foundation of the apostles and prophets, Christ Jesus himself being the cornerstone." Although these offices may have been ephemeral, particularly that of apostle, today's ministers ought to be apostolic in spirit and message and prophetic in preaching.

Evangelists appear in our lists for the first time. The word was lacking in the earlier passages, though it is clear that the apostles were evangelists. By the time Ephesians was written, however, a special class of men was coming into existence whose primary function was to be evangelists, missionaries, proclaimers of the good news.

Pastors and teachers. Though Calvin thought that two offices are set forth here, many present-day scholars believe that the two are one.[28] Charles Hodge rightly said that the two functions cannot be kept separate.[29] The true pastor is also a teacher. The teacher dedicating his life to work in college or seminary or other educational work knows that he is failing if he does not show pastoral concern for those whom he teaches. "Some [to be] pastors and teachers" refers to the local ministry, the preaching elder who settles in a community and ministers to its folk. This is the first clear-cut indication of such an office in the New Testament. The word translated pastor, *poimeinas*, is used only here of Christian teachers, though it is several times applied to our Lord, and a kindred verb form is used at least four times.[30] Professor Stoeckhardt in his commentary on Ephesians says that "By the terms 'pastors and teachers' Paul designates the regular *ministerium verbi* . . . the public office of the ministry of the Word."[31]

The conclusion of this study is that while these lists are primarily and immediately functional, the hints of office grow stronger until with Ephesians we are on the threshold of office, if not across it. The spirit of the ministry is written all through these passages, that he who runs may read. Ephesians sets forth the thought that apostles and prophets were for the founding of the church; the evangelists were to become the proclaimers of the gospel in the church at large and to the world as missionaries; and pastors and teachers were the local pas-

toral ministers of particular congregations. Not even Ephesians answers the question of the threefold ministry or the bishop-presbyter
question. But Ephesians emphasizes the gift of ministry to the church,
and that includes persons called and gifted for the ministerial functions and offices. In his wisdom the Holy Spirit imparts gifts in varying measure; we are responsible for how we receive and use these
gifts.

III

THREE BIBLICAL WORDS:
ELDER, BISHOP, DEACON

In this chapter we shall carry further the discussion of the biblical view of the ministry, completing our brief study of the biblical words. The Bible shows traces of an institutional ministry, especially in the Pastoral Epistles, and of a charismatic ministry, such as tongues, interpretation, and healing. It also gives hints both of a general ministry for the church at large and a ministry for the local church. Biblical usage is so fluid that dogmatic statements cannot fairly be made. At first, apparently, the apostles were roving missionaries or evangelists, and so were some, at least, of the prophets. Many of the functional ministries studied in the preceding chapter were carried out in local churches, but some were possibly more general. While some writers think that teachers had a general ministry, they were probably local leaders. Professor Rudolph Bultmann has an important point: at first the church was so sure the world would end soon that it did not feel the necessity of working out a clear-cut organization, yet because the church existed not simply as an eschatological community but also as a community in time and in history, an organization became inevitable. The fellowship of salvation became an institution of salvation.[1] It is human nature that whenever men gather in community, some organization will follow, some leadership is essential. Local congregations simply had to have some form of organization. There could be no spirit without form, no church without leaders. In time the local church leaders became known as elders, bishops, and deacons.

ELDERS *(Presbyteroi)*

At first the disciples continued to worship God in the Temple, not realizing that a break with the Jewish faith was inevitable. Apparently

35

the church at Jerusalem formed in effect a Christian synagogue within Judaism. Both in form of organization and in form of worship the early church drew heavily upon the ways to which it was accustomed. Jewish communities were governed by a council of elders. The Greek word is *presbyteros*, which may be transliterated presbyter. A single elder was a *presbyteros*, a group of elders were *presbyteroi*, presbytery. The word means elder, old man, a senior male citizen. It was universally believed that wisdom went along with age. The Jewish elders were responsible for the conduct of the business and the charities of the local Jewish community, and for the exercise of discipline in accordance with the law of Moses. The concept of "elder" in the Bible goes back to the time of Moses (Exod. 18) but is far older, for primitive people nearly everywhere have given the aged men of the tribe a large degree of leadership and respect.

Early in its history the church at Jerusalem chose some of its older men as leaders. Relief was dispatched from Antioch "to the elders by the hand of Barnabas and Saul" (Acts 11:30). Elders were strongly in evidence at the Jerusalem Conference, in which they shared in the government of the church with the apostles (Acts 15). Paul and Barnabas appointed elders in the churches which they founded (Acts 14:23 and 20:17).

The elders in the Christian churches probably assumed the prerogatives of the elders in the Jewish synagogues. In addition, however, they were given teaching and pastoral responsibilities. Paul, speaking in farewell to the elders of Ephesus, charged them, "Take heed to yourselves and to all the flock [*poimneo*], in which the Holy Spirit has made you guardians [*episkopous*, bishops], to feed [*poimainein*, to shepherd or to pastor] the church of the Lord which he obtained with his own blood" (Acts 20:28).

Paul, in the epistles which are generally accepted as his, does not use the term elder (presbyter). It is used, however, in James 5:14, where the sick are exhorted to send for the elders of the church, that they may pray for and anoint them with oil. Paul does use the word *proistamenos*, best translated "he who rules" (instead of "gives aid" —Rom. 12:8). The same word is used in the plural, "Respect those who . . . are over you in the Lord" (1 Thess. 5:12). These rulers were almost certainly elders. This same Greek word "to rule" is used explicitly of elders in 1 Timothy 5:17. In Hebrews 13:7, 17, a different Greek word for leader, *hegoumenois*, is used. Elders bear rule in the church!

The Pastoral Epistles, which are Pauline in essence, perhaps based upon notes from Paul and elaborated by a disciple, also speak of elders. Highly important passages are 1 Timothy 5:17-22 and Titus 1:5-9. A key verse in Presbyterian polity is 1 Timothy 5:17: "Let the elders who rule well be considered worthy of double honor, especially those who labor in preaching and teaching." From Calvin on, most Reformed thinkers have taken this verse to imply that there are two kinds of elders, those who rule and those who both teach and rule. Both kinds of elders, apparently, received not only respect but also financial remuneration (1 Tim. 5:18), though today only the teaching elder receives pay for his work, which is now a full-time vocation. Elders are not to be lightly accused, nor are charges to be heard against them upon the evidence of less than two or three witnesses (1 Tim. 5:19).

In a graphic description of the work of an elder, Peter writes:

"So I exhort the elders among you, as a fellow elder and a witness of the sufferings of Christ as well as a partaker in the glory that is to be revealed. Tend the flock of God that is your charge, not by constraint but willingly, not for shameful gain but eagerly, not as domineering over those in your charge but being examples to the flock. And when the chief Shepherd is manifested you will obtain the unfading crown of glory. Likewise you that are younger be subject to the elders. Clothe yourselves . . . with humility toward one another . . ." (1 Peter 5:1-5).

Peter calls himself a fellow elder. The pastor of the writer's boyhood days, when distributing to the ruling elders during Communion, would always say, "I who am an elder with you . . ." Note the phrase, "tend the flock of God." The Greek has it, *poimanate* (shepherd) the *poimenion* (flock) of God. This is pastoral care! The elder serves willingly, not for gain, and he does not lord it over his flock but lives as an example. Christ is called the chief Shepherd. All pastors are undershepherds. In this Petrine passage, elder seems to denote office, age, and function.

Some scholars believe that the author of the book of Revelation was reflecting the church order and the worship of his day when in his visions he spoke of the four and twenty elders seated around the heavenly throne (Rev. 4:4).[2]

In summary, the elders ruled, taught, preached, conducted worship, shepherded the flock, guided in humility, as undershepherds of the great Shepherd. By the end of the first century, or in the generation thereafter, some local congregations were governed by a council of elders or presbyters.[3]

BISHOP *(Episkopos)*

In some churches, it seems, the word *episkopos,* overseer or bishop, was used in place of the word presbyter or elder. Paul greets the bishops and deacons of the church of Philippi (Phil. 1:1). At the beginning there seems to have been no clear distinction between elder and bishop. Protestant scholars point to two key passages. In Acts 20, the elders *(presbyterous)* of verse 17 are addressed as bishops *(episkopous)* ("guardians," RSV) in verse 28.

A significant passage is Titus 1:5-7. ". . . appoint elders in every town as I directed you, if any man is blameless, the husband of one wife, and his children are believers and not open to the charge of being profligate or insubordinate. For a bishop, as God's steward, must be blameless . . ."

While it is possible to work out tortuous arguments to show that these words cannot mean what they seem to mean, most students are willing to admit with Bishop Lightfoot that at the beginning the words bishop and elder were used interchangeably.[4] John Knox suggests that *episkopos* (bishop) was sometimes used to make intelligible to Gentiles the meaning of the Hebrew concept *presbyteros* (elder), which would have sounded strange to them as a title.[5] The term *episkopos* was familiar to Greeks and Romans, who gave this title to the overseer of a club, the man in charge of an organization. A deeper explanation of the usage of overseer and pastor goes back to the Old Testament, notably to the concept of God as shepherd in Psalm 23 and in Ezekiel 34.

In the Pastoral Epistles bishop *(episkopos)* is always mentioned in the singular (1 Tim. 3:1-7; Titus 1:7-9). Many scholars believe that by the time the Pastoral Epistles were written, the church organization had evolved to the point where there was just one bishop in each church. This conclusion is not definite, for even in the Pastoral Epistles the bishop is still one of the elders. We know, from a letter written by Bishop Clement of Rome to the church of Corinth in A.D. 96, that both churches were governed by a council of elders.[6] Clement, presumably one of the elders but also the permanent presiding officer, was a prototype of the local bishop or what we call today the pastor or minister of a congregation.

By this time or shortly thereafter, the elders, and/or bishops, were responsible for the administration of the church as well as for worship and the conduct of the Eucharist.[7] They were expected to be men worthy of the respect to which their office entitled them, for they were servants of a King!

DEACON *(Diakonos)*

Ministry *(diakonia)* and the verb meaning to exercise a ministry *(diakoneo)* occur fairly often in the New Testament, but there are very few references to the office of a minister *(diakonos* or deacon). Acts 6:1-6 is held by most Reformed scholars to be an account of the origin of the diaconate. The apostles felt, as do most ministers today, "It is not right that we should give up preaching the word of God to serve tables" (Acts 6:2). They asked the church at Jerusalem to pick out "seven men of good repute, full of the Spirit and of wisdom" (Acts 6:3), to be appointed for the duty. Among the seven men chosen were Philip the evangelist and Stephen the martyr, both of whom became known for their preaching. The passage implies that the seven were to serve tables, the basic meaning of "to deacon." Some modern students doubt that this really means that these men were deacons, and nowhere in the New Testament are they called "deacons."[8] John Knox has suggested that the seven were Greek-speaking Jews, chosen to give that group representation in the council of elders at Jerusalem.[9]

The church at Philippi had deacons, a word known to the pagan world as a municipal officer or a club official. The deacons were evidently of a lower rank than were the presbyters or bishops (1 Tim.

3:8-13). In later church history, the deacon was the bishop's assistant. The qualifications, and long tradition, hint that the deacon's task was the administration of the charitable funds of the church. Some scholars think the primitive church also had women deacons (Rom. 16:1; 1 Tim. 3:11). It is certain that the deacon was the helper, just as the elder-bishop was the administrator.

THE NEW TESTAMENT CHURCH: IN SUMMARY

In the New Testament church, the apostles, witnesses of the Resurrection, were the chief officers, called and appointed by Christ and given the keys of the Kingdom. Where the apostles established churches, they ordained elders to form a governing council. Greeks, Romans, and Hebrews all knew the meaning of organization and of leadership, and it is psychologically and sociologically probable that there was more firmness to the organization of a particular congregation than many current biblical scholars allow. The more often the Christians assembled, the more certain was an organizational structure to evolve. God set some in the church for certain functions. The ascended Christ gave to the church a ministry. The Twelve symbolized the fact that the church was the new Israel. They had no successors. But the church is apostolic, and all its members, certainly including its ordained ministers, are "sent ones," apostles of the living God.

By the time Ephesians was written, not only were there wandering prophets and traveling teachers, but probably some local congregations had their own pastor-teachers, along with the bishop-presbyter and deacons.[10] All of the leaders, whatever their title, were servants of God, carrying out the ministry of Christ in and through the church.

One thing needs to be added to this account. First Corinthians gives us a picture of a congregation in which the leadership was still largely congregational. Without clear-cut leadership save that of the absent apostle, there was a good deal of confusion. It is possible that the government and worship at Corinth were atypical. At Corinth, apparently, leadership in worship was spontaneous, "Spirit-led." A careful reading of First Corinthians, chapter 14, suggests that Paul was not very happy with the ebullient worship at Corinth. "But all things should be done decently and in order" (14:40). This principle meant, as Clement's letter shows, that even in Corinth, before the end of the first century there would arise a council to govern, perhaps assisted by a diaconate to administer the finances and the charities, and with one man appointed to preside at council meeting and at the Lord's Supper. The extreme freedom from structure and order of the Corinthian church could not continue if the church was to grow. More form and order were a necessity. It is currently popular to talk much of the church as a fellowship, and to scorn the institutional aspect. The church, however, is and will continue to be both a fellowship and an institution.

A SINGLE BISHOP IN A SINGLE CHURCH

When Bishop Clement of Rome wrote in A.D. 96 his oft-quoted, controversial epistle to the church at Corinth, it was because he wanted to help the church at Corinth as it faced internal strife. Certain *episkopoi* (bishops) at Corinth, to be equated with presbyters or elders, had been deposed from office, due to the machinations of some ambitious folk. According to Clement the apostles appointed, as their first-fruits, bishops (elders) and deacons to govern the newly formed churches, including Corinth. In chapter 44 of Clement's epistle there is much ambiguity. He seems to recognize that a corporate presbytery was the original form of church government at Corinth. The arguments revolve around these words:

"Now our apostles . . . knew that there was going to be strife over the title of bishop. . . . they appointed the officers we have mentioned. Furthermore, they later added a codicil to the effect that, should these die, other approved men should succeed to their ministry. In the light of this, we view it as a breach of justice to remove from their ministry those who were appointed either by them [i.e., the apostles] or later on and with the whole church's consent, by others of the proper standing, and who, long enjoying everybody's approval, have ministered to Christ's flock faultlessly, humbly, quietly, and unassumingly."[11] Is the ministry to which these men succeed that of the apostles or of the presbyters? Did the congregation elect the officers who were then appointed, or were they ap-

pointed by the apostles or bishops? Experts on the history of the
primitive church wax hot on these issues. Cyril Richardson recognizes
that Clement still uses presbyter and bishop for the same class of
persons, and that the monepiscopate is not fully established. Richardson, however, sees here the essence of the doctrine of apostolic
succession.[12] K. J. Woollcombe takes a more conciliatory view, noting
that in Clement's letter ". . . the emphasis is all on the succession of
approved men with the consent of the Church."[13]

These hints of the difficulties in this one letter make clear why
Canon Streeter in his study of the primitive church finally concluded
with Alice in Wonderland, "Everyone has won, and all shall have
prizes." "In the Primitive Church no one system of Church Order
prevailed. Everywhere there was readiness to experiment, and, where
circumstances seemed to demand it, to change."[14] In the first post-
biblical records, as well as in the Bible, then, we find ambiguity concerning the ministry. Fairly early, the church had a duly recognized
ministry. Seeds of all the major forms of church government—
episcopal, congregational, and presbyterial—may be discerned. While
Christ gave his church the ministry, he did not give it a particular
form of church government. The ministry in its visible form and its
specific functions may well vary with the changing circumstances of
the passing years. But a ministry there must be, and its basic loyalty
and its primary message are always the same: "Jesus Christ is Lord."
That ministry must not be treated irreverently or deposed without
just cause.

The first clear indication of a single bishop (monepiscopacy) or
pastor (minister) at the head of a particular church occurs in the
writings of Ignatius, Bishop of Antioch in Syria. In A.D. 112 Ignatius
advised the church at Smyrna, "All of you follow the bishop as Jesus
Christ followed the Father, and follow the presbytery as the Apostles;
and respect the deacons as the commandment of God. Let no man
perform anything pertaining to the church without the bishop."[15]
The bishop in Smyrna conducts the Eucharist and symbolizes Jesus
Christ to the world. By the time of Ignatius, then, at least some of the
churches of Asia Minor were governed by a bench of elders presided
over by a bishop. Whether the bishop was simply one of the presbyters who was elected by his fellow presbyters (Bishop Lightfoot, and

the Reformed Church in general) or whether he was appointed by a fellow bishop and heir to the apostolic succession (Catholics of all varieties), we do not know. In any case, by the Council of Nicea, A.D. 325, practically all Christendom had the monepiscopate, that is, a local bishop or pastor with his bench of elders.

By the time of Irenaeus, *circa* A.D. 150, diocesan bishops had appeared, men who were ranked above the local bishops and had charge of a diocese. Fifty years later Tertullian made clear distinction between bishops and presbyters. Cyprian (d. 258), martyr bishop of the church in North Africa, put the claims of episcopacy in high church fashion: ". . . the bishop is in the Church and the Church in the bishop, and . . . if anyone be not with the bishop he is not in the Church."[16] Cyprian's bishops took no important actions without the consent and advice of their presbyters. For a long time the bishops were of equal rank. Inasmuch as each congregation had its bishop, the men in charge of the great city churches, in that day as in ours, assumed a natural leadership, sometimes warranted. A hierarchy gradually developed among the bishops. Lowest were the country bishops, pastors of rural churches and mission stations, who were taken under the wing of the bishop of the nearby city. The time came when there was one bishop for each city, with a presbyter (now rapidly becoming a priest in the current Roman Catholic sense) in charge of each particular congregation. This development cannot be precisely dated, but it was a natural unfolding of the concept of the bishop as the man who was to unify the church, to be the depository of the apostolic tradition, the defender of the orthodox faith, and the vice-regent of Christ in spiritual affairs. The metropolitan bishops, dwelling in the provincial capitals, came to be thought of as presiding officers at the provincial synods, and as ordainers of the bishops of the provinces. The bishops of Jerusalem, Rome, Alexandria, and Antioch were of especial prominence. In time they became known as patriarchal bishops.

As early as A.D. 100, the church at Rome was beginning to show signs of a sense of superiority, and a century later the Roman bishop, Victor, in his own name excommunicated the churches of Asia Minor for an unimportant ritual difference.[17] The rise of the papacy was under way. The view which the Roman Church holds concerning the place and power of the Pope had its roots in political and in psychological more than in theological soil.[18]

THE YEARS OF ROMANIZATION

The twelve hundred years from Nicea to the beginning of the Protestant Reformation in 1517 were marked by growing sacerdotalism. Presbyters became priests. The three orders of ministry—the diaconate, the presbyterate, and the episcopate—became rigidly defined, separate classes. Lower orders of sub-clergy abounded. The Council of Laodicea in A.D. 380 expressly forbade the election of a bishop by the people. Though Jerome and others of the early church fathers argued that bishops were but presbyters with greater jurisdiction and the power of ordination, a great change took place when the bishop thought of his ministry as a distinct and separate order. The bishops during this long period of church history gained in power, authority, privilege, and duties. The tonsure became the hallmark of the clergy in the fourth century. By A.D. 350 many of the clergy were wearing a distinctive garb. Accepting the view of Greek philosophy that the body is evil rather than the biblical view that sex is a gift of God as part of his creation, churchmen came to think it incompatible for those who had sex relations to offer up the holy sacrifice. Very slowly the clergy accepted celibacy.[19] By the twelfth century, however, the principle of celibacy prevailed.

With the rise of the monastic orders, the clergy were divided into two groups, the regular clergy, the monks regulated by the monastic rules, and the "secular" clergy who served *in saeculo*, in the world. Roland Bainton shows in fascinating fashion that, although the church fathers had made it clear that "The minister then should not be a merchant, a magistrate, or a militiaman," during the Middle Ages he became all three.[20]

During this long period there were some great Christian men who served the church. Three of them wrote able books on the work of the pastor. Chrysostom wrote *On the Priesthood, circa* A.D. 386. He was sure that ". . . the pre-eminent qualification of the true pastor was his readiness to perish for his sheep."[21] Ambrose in A.D. 386 wrote *On the Duty of Ministers*, stressing a high view of the episcopate, and of the loyalty of the priest to his Lord. Gregory the Great's volume, *Pastoral Care*,[22] is full of sound insights.

In this long, dim period, the simple view of the minister as a servant of Christ and the people became lost or at least perverted. Some clergymen of the Middle Ages of course gave magnificent service, but too many were mediocre little men, ignorant, uneducated, perhaps doing their feeble best. And some were in the ministry for what they could get out of it. Powerful secular lords through the process of lay investiture placed their favorites in positions of wealth and leadership in the church. Perhaps most of the clergy were good men, but preaching was mediocre, teaching weak, and even pastoral care often was poorly done. Sacerdotal functions were better cared for.

The tragedy of these long years is that during them the clergy and the laity became separated from each other to a marked degree. It was not simply a matter of clothing, haircut, and celibacy in name or in fact. At the very core of the life of the church a barrier was erected. Only the priest could enter the sanctuary proper; only he communed in both kinds; only he could excommunicate; only he pronounced, *"Absolvo te."* He gained a power over the lives of his people that no man has a right to wield. Priestly absolution was taken by ignorant folk to be the personal power of their priest to forgive or to withhold forgiveness, whereas its real meaning was that only Christ forgives and the minister simply announces the fact. It is good for a Christian to respect the judgment of his minister concerning a spiritual or moral problem, but to live one's life in fear of what the priest may say is quite a different thing. The sharp division of Christian people into two classes, clergy and laity, was a colossal error in the history of the church. That breach may be repaired in our time!

IV

THE EARLY CONTINENTAL
REFORMERS ON THE MINISTRY

When Martin Luther made his protest against the scandalous sale of indulgences, the church was priest-ridden. The ecclesiastical hierarchy was far too powerful. The Mass was too literally conceived as a sacrifice, in which the priest "made God." Priests were much too sharply separated from laymen, and they had assumed prerogatives which no man has a right to claim. Once a reformation began, the concept of the ministry was certain to be changed. The long forgotten concept of the priesthood of believers was revived, and the clergy were recognized to be part of the laity (*laos*—the people) of God.

MARTIN LUTHER

Augustinian monk, learned Doctor of the church, great preacher, and sparkplug of the Reformation, Martin Luther was a picture of the changing concept of the ministry in his time. After his break with Rome, Luther considered much of the ritual of the liturgy a matter of indifference. What the minister wears makes no difference, but what he preaches and how he lives are important. Luther ignored his monastic vows and married Katherine von Bora and encouraged other former priests and nuns to marry. In his own life as a leader of the Reformation, Luther wielded a personal power far greater than that of many a bishop in the Roman Catholic Church. His power was that of a natural leader, not one assumed by right of office. One only has to dip into his *Table Talk* or read some of his pastoral letters to realize the amazing influence of the man. He gave his personal judgments fearlessly. He counseled large numbers of persons, lay and ministerial, as though he were a bishop. Yet it was he who brought alive the concept of the priesthood of believers.

Luther's concept of the ministry was rooted in the church as a society of believers. Every believer in Christ is himself a priest, a minister, an evangelist, a teacher; for Christ, who in his own Person was all of these, has given it to his body, the church, to carry out these functions in its life (1 Peter 2: 4-10). "We are all priests, insofar as we are Christians, but those whom we call priests are ministers [*Diener*] selected from our midst to act in our name, and their priesthood is our ministry."[1] For the sake of good order, the church must have an ordained clergy set apart by the body for this purpose. In principle, this wiped out the barrier between clergy and laity. The priestly hierarchy was done away with, and men could talk with their ministers without fear. All ministers are part of the *laos*. Baptism is the ordination of the laity into the priesthood of believers.[2]

"The principle of mutual guidance and spiritual stimulation is as old as the New Testament . . . It rests upon the belief that the gifts of the Spirit move through the whole membership of the Church, and that, in no merely theoretic sense, all Christians are functioning members of one living body, exercising toward one another a spiritual or priestly office."[3]

Luther had a high view of the ministry as well as of the church. Wilhelm Pauck has summarized this effectively: "[The Reformers] . . . regarded the function of the leader of the congregation, whose task was to be primarily preaching, as an assignment or office [*Amt*] which, to be sure, set him apart from his fellow Christians but only by their appointment, in order that he might perform a duty that each one of them was entitled to fulfill. Moreover, they regarded this office as a service to be rendered in the name of God and not in the name of men. Once appointed to the office, a minister could not be removed from it by the congregation that had called him, except if he disregarded or defied the Word of God."[4]

The wall was down; clergy and laity were on a par. Yet Luther knew that some differentiation was necessary. At Luther's home on November 25, 1538, "there was talk about the perpetual enmity between the clergy and the laity." Anthony Lauterbach, the recorder, then summarizes: " 'It is not without cause,' said Martin Luther, 'since the untamed masses are unwilling to be corrected and it is the duty of preachers to reprove them. This is a very burdensome and perilous duty. And on this account laymen keep sharp eyes on clergymen. They try to find some fault in them, and if they discover a grievous offense, even if it be in the clergymen's wives or children, they are delighted to have their revenge on them. Except that they surpass other people in power, princes harass clergymen with a like hatred. Let us therefore adhere to the pure Word in order that we may sit in the seat of Moses. . . . Enmity toward clergymen will remain. As the old saying puts it, 'Not until the sea dries up and the devil is taken up into heaven will the layman be a true friend of the clergyman.' "5

To Conrad Cordatus, who had been ordered by the town council of Zwickau to stop preaching after he had publicly scolded the people and attacked the town council from the pulpit, Luther wrote: ". . . if you continue to minister to these unwilling, impenitent, and desperate people, you may irritate them even more and give them additional cause to hate you. Flee from that town . . . As good pastors [Nicholas Hausmann as well as Cordatus], you cannot refrain from rebuking people's wickedness. But since they refuse to listen to and heed your reproaches, let them rage on. . . ."6

Luther wrote in exaggerated fashion, of course. He knew that ministers as well as laymen could be poor Christians. Writing to Prince George of Anhalt, July 10, 1545, he said of some ministers: "But only a few are willing to study, while many are concerned only with their bellies and a place where they might be fed. Hence it has occurred to me more than once that it may become necessary to decrease the number of village pastors and to employ, in lieu of several such pastors, just one learned and faithful man who might visit all the places in a neighborhood several times a year to provide pure preaching and diligent supervision; meanwhile the people might repair to the mother church for the Sacraments or, in case of illness, have the deacons administer the Sacraments to them. Time and circumstances will suggest what cannot be fixed or predetermined by laws."7

Luther knew full well that as long as a man faithfully preaches the Word of God, he will offend sinful men. Preaching was the primary task of the minister, according to Luther and the other Reformers, and in his capacity as a preacher, the minister must be treated with respect. When he preaches the gospel, we can forget that he is a man whose feet are made of clay. Luther said, "The preaching office is the office of the Holy Spirit. Even though men do the preaching, baptizing, forgiving of sins, it is the Holy Spirit who preaches and teaches. It is his work and office."[8]

JOHN CALVIN

The great French Reformer, like Luther, had a high view of the minister's place in the church. To Calvin, the minister was primarily a man called of God rather than a man set apart by the people. This is perhaps an oversimplification. Luther did not deny the call of God, but he stressed the lifting up from the total priesthood of a few for ministerial office. Calvin did not deny the priesthood of believers, but he emphasized the ministry as a gift from God to the church.

Book IV of the *Institutes* is entitled, "The External Means or Aids by Which God Invites Us Into the Society of Christ and Holds Us Therein." Chapter three is on "The Doctors and Ministers of the Church, Their Election and Office." Calvin begins by saying that the Lord has willed an order for the government of the church. "He alone should rule and reign in the church as well as have authority or pre-eminence in it, and this authority should be exercised and administered by his Word alone. . . . he uses the ministry of men to declare openly his will to us by mouth, as a sort of delegated work, not by transferring to them his right and honor, but only that through their mouths he may do his own work—just as a workman uses a tool to do his work."[9] Instead of intervening directly, or using angels, God shows his regard for us when "from among men he takes some to serve as his ambassadors in the world [cf. II Cor. 5:20], to be interpreters of his secret will and, in short, to represent his person."[10] This is an exercise in humility, "when he accustoms us to obey his Word, even though it be preached through men like us and sometimes even by those of lower worth than we. . . . Further, nothing fosters mutual love more fittingly than for men to be bound together with this bond: one is appointed pastor to teach the rest, and those bidden to be pupils receive the common teaching from one mouth.

For if anyone were sufficient to himself and needed no one else's help (such is the pride of human nature), each man would despise the rest and be despised by them. . . ."[11]

Discussing Ephesians 4:4-16, Calvin comments that the ascended Christ fills "all things." ". . . through the ministers to whom he has entrusted this office and has conferred the grace to carry it out, he dispenses and distributes his gifts to the church; and he shows himself as though present by manifesting the power of his Spirit in this his institution, that it be not vain or idle. . . . Whoever, therefore, either is trying to abolish this order of which we speak and this kind of government, or discounts it as not necessary, is striving for the undoing or rather the ruin and destruction of the church. For neither the light and heat of the sun, nor food and drink, are so necessary to nourish and sustain the present life as the apostolic and pastoral office is necessary to preserve the church on earth."[12]

Calvin sees two classes of ministers in the Bible, temporary (apostles, prophets, and evangelists) and permanent (pastors and teachers). The teaching office he sees to be that of "Scriptural interpretation—to keep doctrine whole and pure among believers," while the pastoral office includes within itself teaching, preaching, administration of sacraments, and discipline.[13] Although all ministers may be called apostles, "because all are sent by the Lord and are his messengers," the pastors preside over particular churches. Administration of the sacraments and preaching are the two main functions of the pastor, but Calvin includes private admonition in pastoral visitation as part of preaching (see Acts 20:21, 31). Pastors have been set over the church "not to have a sinecure but, by the doctrine of Christ to instruct the people to true godliness, to administer the sacred mysteries and to keep and exercise upright discipline."[14] Calvin believes firmly that each pastor should be assigned to his own church and should never invade the parish of another (vs. the sectaries).[15] When a man has received a divine call to a particular church, he should not leave the post unless the public benefit require, and he should never think of leaving simply for his own advantage.[16] If expedience seems to indicate that he should move elsewhere, he should be guided by public authority.

Government and care of the poor were meant to be permanent

functions. Governors were elders. The care of the poor was committed to deacons. Curiously, Calvin sees two kinds of deacons in Romans 12:8. One class dispenses the alms given for the poor, the other class, including women, takes care of the poor and sick. This unusual interpretation covers two basic functions of the modern Presbyterian diaconate, charity and social welfare, but it does not include the administration of church finances and the care of church property.[17]

All things in the church are to be done decently and in order. "Therefore, in order that noisy and troublesome men should not rashly take upon themselves to teach or to rule (which might otherwise happen), especial care was taken that no one should assume public office in the church without being called."[18] By call Calvin means a solemn external call from the church. A secret call, of which each minister is conscious before God, is assumed.[19] Those whom the Lord has destined to so important an office as the ministry, "he first supplies with the arms required to fulfill it . . ."[20] The church is to choose only godly, able men. The choice of a minister is to be made with religious awe, in fasting and prayer. Calvin interprets "appointed" in Acts 14:23 as election by raising the hand, so he believes Paul and Barnabas to have been ordained after the election by the people. He agrees with Cyprian that public election of the bishop and public approval of his worth and fitness for the office are of divine origin.[21]

"We therefore hold that this call of a minister is lawful according to the Word of God, when those who seemed fit are created by the consent and approval of the people; moreover, that other pastors ought to preside over the election in order that the multitude may not go wrong either through fickleness, through evil intentions, or through disorder."[22]

Following the apostolic example, ordination is to be by imposition of hands by one or more ministers.[23]

Calvin considers the minister to have great authority, but he does not believe in a priestly hierarchy as a source of authority. The authority of the minister is not in his own character, nor his own gracious personality, nor even his election by the people, all of which have genuine value, but is solely the authority of the Word of God.

Professor A. Dakin states it well: "Since Christ is the head of the Church, the minister's chief business is to maintain that authority, and any authority and power conferred by the Holy Spirit . . . is but a delegated authority, and belongs to the office and not to the men themselves."[24] Though Calvin dared to say that by his ministry Christ ruled His flock, "He knew, of course, that the authority and dignity of the office did not spring from the man to whom it is committed. This authority and dignity are rather inherent in the office itself, or better still in the Word of God, to serve which the person concerned is called."[25]

This high doctrine of the ministry is rooted in a high doctrine of the church, which to Calvin was "the mother of believers, the body of Christ." When Calvin returned to Geneva in 1541, he wrote the famous *Ordonnances Ecclesiastiques*, with the final draft showing many compromises forced by the town council. Believing that the Bible sets forth *de jure* a form of church order, Calvin provided for four church offices: pastors, teachers ("Doctors"), elders, and deacons. The office of the pastors is "to proclaim the Word of God, to instruct, admonish, exhort and censure, both in public and private, to administer the sacraments and to enjoin brotherly corrections along with the elders and colleagues."[26] The pastors as a body examined prospective pastors and recommended them to congregations. "Candidates for the pastoral office must give proof of their vocation to it, first by passing a test in doctrine and being approved in conduct, and second through the stages of presentation by the ministers, acceptance by the Little Council, and consent of the people. The imposition of hands, though held to be apostolic, is for the time omitted because of then current superstition regarding its use."[27] There was a provision for weekly discussion meetings of the ministers of Geneva and the villages nearby. Where doctrinal disagreements arose, elders were to be called in; if they failed to bring unity, then the magistrates were to pronounce judgments. (The magistrates, not the Consistory, held the final authority in Geneva.) The ministers met quarterly as the Venerable Company for mutual discipline.

The "Doctors" (teachers) were to instruct the people in true doctrine. They were also to train men for the ministry. This led to the establishment of a college. They were chosen by the ministers, with the approval of the Council.

The twelve ruling elders were chosen from, and by, the magistrates. "Their office is to have oversight of the life of everyone, to admonish amicably those whom they see to be erring or to be living a disordered life, and, where it is required, to enjoin fraternal corrections themselves . . ."[28] The pastors joined the ruling elders in church discipline. The twelve elders, together with the pastors, constituted the Consistory. The city was divided into districts, cared for by pastors and elders specifically assigned. The two kinds of deacons were elected in the same manner as the elders.

This church order became "the most influential of all that were produced by the Reformation."[29] It became the foundation of the church order of all later Presbyterian and Reformed churches, notably in France, Holland, Hungary, Scotland, and America.

ZWINGLI AND BULLINGER

Huldreich Zwingli (1484-1531) wrote his treatise, *The Pastor*, in March 1524. It spoke directly to priests who were in the throes of deciding whether to cast their lot with the Reformation. The prophet's office (the heavenly teaching) will always be continued in the church. The power of the keys is to be found primarily in the preaching of the Word; on this point Zwingli agreed with all the Reformers. Zwingli organized at Zurich a synod which met twice a year, to supervise the doctrine and morals of the people, and to govern the life of the church. Its membership was composed of all the ministers of city and canon, two lay representatives from each parish, and eight members from the government. This synod had two presidents, a minister and a layman. The distinction between laymen and ministers is one of function. "It is true we are all fully ordained to the priesthood which in the New Testament offers sacrifices, which means nothing else but that everyone offers himself. But we are not all apostles and bishops."[30]

Heinrich Bullinger was Zwingli's successor at Zurich. He was less original and more systematic than his predecessor. In a lengthy sermon, "Of the Holy Catholic Church," he set forth his ideas on the nature and work of pastors. "The Lord himself appointed the first doctors of the Church, the apostles, in order that all men might understand that the ecclesiastical ministry is the divine institution of

God himself, and not a tradition devised by men. . . . But if the Church has received power to appoint suitable ministers for the Church, I do not think that there are any who will deny that it has the authority to depose the unworthy and wicked deceivers, and also to correct and amend . . .

"And since ministers are chosen chiefly to teach, it follows necessarily that the Church has power to teach, to exhort, to comfort and such like by means of its lawful ministers: yet not the power to teach everything, but only that which it received as delivered from the Lord by the doctrine of the prophets and apostles. . . . Canonical truth teaches us that Christ himself holds and exercises absolute or full power in the Church, and that he has given ministerial power to the Church, which executes it for the most part by ministers, and religiously executes it according to the rule of God's Word."[31]

THE PROTESTANT COUNCILS

The various Protestant Councils during the Reformation years issued statements revealing a lofty evaluation of the place of the ministers of Word and Sacrament in the life of the church. We give three samples.

"The Apostles of Christ indeed call all believers in Christ priests, but not by reason of a ministerial office, but because through Christ all who are the faithful, having been made kings and priests, are able to offer spiritual sacrifices to God. Accordingly, there are great differences between a priesthood and a ministry. For the former is common to all Christians . . . but the same is not so with the latter. And we have not removed the ministry out of the midst of the Church when we have cast the papistical priesthood out of the Church of Christ." (Second Helvetic Confession, 1566.)[32]

"Thus we receive the true ministers of the Word of God as messengers and ambassadors of God, to whom it is required to hearken as to Himself, and we consider their ministry is a commission from God necessary in the Church." (Genevan Confession, 1537.)[33]

In the French Confession of 1599 we read: "Now because we rejoice in Jesus Christ . . . we believe that the order of the Church which has been established by His authority, ought to be sacred and inviolable. And, moreover, the Church is not able to hold together if it has not pastors who have the charge of teaching, whom one ought to honour and hear with reverence when they are duly called, and exercise faithfully their office. Not that God is bound to such lower help and means, but because it pleases Him to maintain us under such charge and control. Wherefore we abhor all fantastic people who greatly desire, so far as it lies with them, to abolish the ministry and the preaching of the Word of God and His sacraments." (Article XXV.) [34]

IN SUMMARY

The Reformers were agreed in teaching that the head of the church is Jesus Christ. The church carries out his ministry. To this end, she ordains ministers of Word and Sacrament. These ministers are primarily preachers of the Word, and when they unfold the gospel, they are to be heeded. The church cannot exist for long without a ministry duly set apart. Ministers are priests only in the sense that all believers are priests; they share in the royal priesthood of the church and they offer up themselves to God. Ministers are to be chosen with utmost care and fully trained. (Calvin in particular emphasized this.) Never for a moment did the Reformers consider their ministry to be less valid than that of the sacrificing priesthood which owed its allegiance to Rome.

V

———··⟨∞⟩··———

THE REFORMED MINISTRY
IN THE BRITISH ISLES

Our primary emphasis will be given to Scotland, with brief consideration of Episcopal and Independent ministries. The histories of Scotland and England during the sixteenth and seventeenth centuries are involved and interrelated. Although to most Americans this history means little, some of the decisions reached during this time probably will slow down current plans for union of certain great denominations.

THE SETTING

For approximately the first hundred years of the Reformation, England was governed by the Tudor line. In the Act of Supremacy, 1534, Henry VIII flatly asserted that he, not the Pope, was the head of the Church of England. During Henry's reign England remained largely Catholic in doctrine and practice without allegiance to Rome. The Church of England adhered to the threefold order of the ministry: bishops, priests, and deacons. This meant that "the bishops rule the ministers and the king rules both." Henry decreed that every English church should have a Bible in the vernacular, thus helping England to become "the people of the Book." During the reign of the youthful Edward VI, 1547-1553, the influence of the Reformation was powerfully felt in England. The liturgical genius, Thomas Cranmer, was primarily responsible for preparing the Book of Common Prayer, which continues to frame the religious devotion of millions. The First Prayer Book of King Edward VI, 1549, was based on the old Rite of Sarum, and could be given a Roman Catholic interpretation. The Second Prayer Book of King Edward VI, 1552, was far more

Protestant in tone, and, slightly revised in 1559, became the Book of Common Prayer.

Queen Mary Tudor I (1553-1558) was Roman Catholic, and many stalwart Protestants fled to the Continent during her reign. Queen Elizabeth I, during her long reign, 1558-1603, was a firm believer in the divine right of the sovereign to rule church as well as state. Under her rule, the Church of England took definite form. The Bible, the Thirty-Nine Articles, and the Book of Common Prayer became basic to the life of this national church. During the intricate history of these years, the Presbyterians, led by Thomas Cartwright of Cambridge, were on the verge of becoming the national church. Like the Anglicans, they favored a national church, but they wanted the Presbyterian system. They insisted that the presbyter had all of the powers of the bishop, for in the Bible and in the early church the two were one office. The combination of theological intransigence and political shifts and turns kept things stirred up. England became Episcopal, while her northern neighbor, Scotland, became Presbyterian.

Under the Tudors, the church remained Catholic, but with Protestant overtones, and free from Rome. Scotland, under the Stuarts, became Presbyterian. The Reformation came to Scotland in 1560. John Knox, a former priest who had accepted Reformed teaching, was forced to flee to Geneva. There he ministered to the English-speaking church, and became an ardent disciple of John Calvin. In 1560 he came back to lead the Reformation in his native land. Several "lairds of the congregation," with political as well as religious interests, helped to make Scotland Presbyterian.

In 1603 James VI of Scotland became the first Stuart king of England, James I, and reigned over the two kingdoms, 1603-1625. In England he was head of the Church of England, in Scotland he was an honored member of the Church of Scotland. The Stuarts were charming but self-centered and untrustworthy rulers. James VI sought to "suppress Puritanism in England, and to anglicise the Northern Church."[1] In 1604 he postponed the meeting of the Scottish Assembly, thus violating its rights. Two years later he imprisoned Andrew Melville, Knox's successor, and soon afterward restored episcopacy to Scotland. A "packed" Assembly in 1610 acknowledged the

king's rule over the church and declared that bishops were superior
to presbyters. In that year, Bishops Spottiswoode, Lamb, and Hamilton received episcopal consecration. They were not reordained, however, for they insisted upon the validity of their orders as presbyters.
(This has been a key point in Presbyterian arguments with Anglicans
to this day.) The three bishops then consecrated their fellow bishops
without reordination. In 1625 the more tolerant Charles I was
crowned king. He was, however, under the influence of Archbishop
Laud, who was determined to force a prayer book upon Scotland.
The Scots did not object to prescribed forms of worship, as Knox's
Liturgy testifies, but they rebelled at having this particular book thrust
upon them. So came the revolt! The Glasgow Assembly of 1638 voted
to eliminate bishops and return to Presbyterianism, despite the objections of the "Aberdeen Doctors." They entered the National
Covenant to defend the church, to oust episcopacy, and to deny
rebellion. In the ensuing years episcopacy again was forced upon
Scotland, and the Covenanters were persecuted, a few being martyred.
With the memory of these tragic years, the Scottish people acquired
a deep loathing of episcopacy. They were more convinced than ever
that a parish bishop (teaching elder) is equal in order to a diocesan
bishop.

THE SCOTTISH VIEW OF THE MINISTRY

The Book of Common Order of the English Kirk at Geneva

The Scottish view of the ministry is a direct outgrowth of the
views of the continental Reformers, particularly John Calvin. The
years John Knox spent in Geneva were all-important for the future
of Scotland. One page of Dunlop's *Collection of Confessions of Faith
... of Publick Authority in the Church of Scotland,* Volume II, 1722,
tells the story. *"The Book of Common Order* or the Order of the
English Kirk at *Geneva,* whereof *John Knox* was Minister: Approved
by the famous and learned Man *John Calvin.* Received and Used by
the Reformed Kirk of *Scotland. . . ."*[2] The preface of this *Book of
Common Order* is inscribed "To our Brethren in England and elsewhere, which love Jesus Christ unfainedly, Mercy and Peace." Dated
February 10, 1556, this preface is a clarion call to the way of the

Reformation. Chapter one, "Of the Ministers and Their Election," states that the minister (pastor) must be a worthy person, who is to distribute faithfully the Word of God, and minister the Sacraments sincerely,[3] teaching his flock both publicly and privately. To have charge of God's Word is a great responsibility, but the minister is not to lord it over his flock; in political affairs his counsel but not his authority may well be sought; and if the congregation decides to excommunicate a person, the minister pronounces the sentence. When pastors (ministers) need to be elected, the ministers and elders call the whole congregation together for advice as to who may best serve in that office. Candidates are examined by ministers and elders, upon their knowledge of doctrine and Scripture, and upon their ability to communicate this knowledge through a trial sermon (privately), as well as upon their manner of life. The man whose gifts seem best suited for that particular church is recommended to the congregation. The people are given eight days in which to inquire into the candidate's life and manners. If all is well, a day is appointed for his election and installation.

Chapter two deals with the elders, who are to be good men, elected in a manner similar to the election of ministers. "In assembling the People, neither they without the Ministers, nor the Ministers without them, may attempt any Thing."[4]

The deacons, elected by the ministers and elders, must have the biblical virtues (1 Tim. 3:8-13). In distributing alms to the needy, the deacons are enjoined to have ever "a diligent Care, that the Charitie of godly Men be not wasted upon Loyterers and ydle Vagabondes."[5] Following Calvin, the office of Teacher or Doctor is described.

The weekly assembly of church officers is like that in Geneva. "To the Intent that the Ministerie of God's Worde may be had in Reverence, and not brought to Contempt through the evill Conversation of such as are called thereunto; and also that Faultes and Vices may not by long Sufferance growe at length to extreame Inconveniences; it is ordeined, that every *Thursday* the Ministers and Elders in their Assembly or Consistorie diligently examine all such Faults and Suspicions as may be espied, not only amongst others, but chiefly amongst themselves, lest they seeme to be culpable of that which our Saviour

Christ reproved in the Pharisees, who could *espie a Mote in another Man's Eye, and could not see a Beame in their own.*

"And because the Eye ought to be more cleare than the rest of the Bodie, the Minister may not be spotted with anie Vice, to the great Slander of God's Worde, whose Message he beareth. . . ."[6] Some faults are so great that for them the minister must be deposed, namely, "Heresie, Papistrie, Schisme, Blasphemie, Perjurie, Fornication, Theft, Drunkennesse, Usurie, Fighting, unlawfull Games, with such like."[7] More tolerable faults for which the minister is to be admonished and given opportunity to amend include "strange and unprofitable Fashion in preaching the Scriptures, Curiositie in seeking vain Questions, Negligence, as well in his Sermons, and in studying the Scriptures, as in all other Things concerning his Vocation, Scurrilitie, Flattering, Lying, Backe-biting . . . which Vices, as they be odious in all Men, so in him, that ought to be as an Example to others of Perfection, in no wise are to be suffered. . . ."[8]

The chapter on church discipline is written with a keen understanding of human weakness and of the need of God's people to be merciful. Discipline is essential for the purity of the church and for the welfare of the weak and sinful. If a matter concerns the whole church, then it should be "uttered to the Ministers and Seniors, to whom the Policy of the Church did appertaine."[9]

The seeds of most that follows in Presbyterian polity are to be found in this brief book of common order. Here is a high view of the ministry. Ministers are to be examined by other ministers and elders, approved by the people, and installed with prayer. Ministers should lead exemplary lives.

The First Book of Discipline, Church of Scotland, 1560

Tradition says that this document was drawn up by the famous "Six Johns" in seven days. These six founding fathers, all former priests, John Winram, John Spottiswood, John Willock, John Douglasse, John Row, and John Knox, actually had spent weeks revising Knox's Genevan Book of Common Order. Chapter four, "Concerning Ministers and Their Lawfull Election," is foundational.

"1. In a Church reformed, or tending to Reformation, none ought to presume either to preach, or yet to minister the Sacraments, till that orderly they be called to the same. Ordinarie Vocation consisteth in Election, Examination, and Admission. . . .

"2. It appertaineth to the People, and to every severall Congregation to elect their Minister." (If a church be vacant for forty days, then the Superintendent with his Councell may present unto them a Man deemed fit for the church.) [10]

The ministers were to be examined publicly, "in all the chiefe Points that now be in Controversie betwixt us and the Papists, Anabaptists, Arrians, or other such Enemies to the Christian religion. . . ."[11] A candidate, approved as godly and capable, preached a trial sermon. If the church could produce no better candidate, then they had to accept the man suggested by the Superintendent's Council. A basic principle is here involved. "For altogether this is to be avoided, that any Man be violently intruded or thrust in upon any Congregation; but this Libertie with all Care must be reserved to every severall Church, to have their Votes and Suffrages in Election of their Ministers. . . ."[12]

A man is disqualified from the ministry when he is "noted with publique Infamie, or being unable to edifie the Church by wholesome Doctrine, or being known of corrupt Judgement. . . ."[13] By public infamy is meant capital crimes. The church is to seek letters of reference for the proposed minister from the community in which he was reared and the place where he was nourished.

"The Admission of Ministers to their Offices must consist in the Consent of the People and Church whereto they shall be appointed, and Approbation of the learned Ministers appointed for their Examination."[14]

Following the public examination, there was to be the equivalent of our present service of installation. The minister is charged that: ". . . with all carefull Diligence [he will] attend upon the Flock of Christ Jesus, over the which he is appointed Pastor; that he will walke in the Presence of God so sincerely, that the Graces of the holy [*sic*] Spirit may be multiplied into him, and in the Presence of Men so soberly and uprightly, that his Life may confirme in the Eyes of Men, that which by Tongue and Word he perswaded unto others. The People should be exhorted to reverence and honor their Ministers chosen, as the Servants and Ambassadors of the Lord Jesus, obeying the Commandements which they pronounce from God's Word, even as they would obey God himselfe: For whosoever heareth Christ's Ministers, heareth himself; and whosoever rejecteth and despiseth their Ministerie and Exhortation, rejecteth and despiseth Christ Jesus."[15]

Perhaps too much has been made of paragraph ten by scholars with low church tendencies. "Other Ceremonie then the publick Approbation of the People, and Declaration of the chiefe Minister, that the Person there presented is appointed to serve the Church, we cannot approve; for albeit the Apostles used Imposition of Hands, yet seeing the Miracle is ceased, the using of the Ceremonie we judge not necessarie."[16] Professor Hugh Watt emphasized the fact that within six years after the First Book of Discipline the Church of Scotland had approved the *Second Helvetic Confession,* which sets forth the laying on of hands as normal at ordination.[17]

Once a minister is installed in a church, he may not leave it at his own pleasure, though he may be transferred by the whole church (presbytery in our modern sense) to another pastorate. Nor may "the Flock reject or change him at their Appetite. . . ."[18]

The Scottish Reformers valued highly an able and godly ministry. There were only a handful of ministers available and most of the thousand or so parishes had become vacant, for a great many of the former priests were unacceptable. The Six Johns believed that it was better to have no minister at all than to have an unworthy one who could not proclaim the Word of God. They were not willing to believe that because a man thinks he has a call from God to preach, the church is bound to accept him as a minister. They insisted that only good and able men would do.

"We are not ignorant that the Raritie of godly and learned Men, will seem to some a just Reason why that so strait and sharpe Examination should not be taken universally; for so it would appear, that the most Part of the Kirks shall have no Minister at all: But let these Men understand, that the Lack of able Men shall not excuse us before God, if by our Consent unable Men be placed over the Flock of Christ Jesus; . . . let them understand that it is alike to have no Minister at all, and to have an Idoll in the Place of a true Minister, yea, and in some Case it is worse; for those that be utterly destitute of Ministers will be diligent to search for them, but those that have a vain Shadow, do commonly without further Care content themselves with the same, and so remain they continually deceived, thinking that they have a Minister when in verie Deed they have none; for we cannot judge him a Dispensator of God's Mysteries, that in no wise can breake the Bread of Life to the fainting and hungrie Soules; neither judge we that the Sacraments can be rightlie ministred by him, in whose Mouth God hath put no Sermon of Exhortation."[19] If a man cannot preach the Word, he ought not to be called a minister! Martin Luther in his famous epistle to the Bohemian Senate, *Concerning the Ministry,* took a similar view.[20]

The Six Johns suggested a remedy for the lack of able men: pray for more men for the ministry. And "the Lordes of the Realme" were asked to "compel" highly qualified men, if called by the church, to set apart their gifts for the preaching of the gospel.

Provision was also made for readers, to read distinctly the common prayers from Knox's Book of Common Order, and the Scriptures. If these readers grew in spiritual ability and zeal, they would be permitted to administer the sacraments and to preach. If they failed to grow, they ceased to be readers. Many of the readers were former priests, some of whom failed to make the grade.

The Second Buik of Discipline (1578)

This book, largely the work of Andrew Melville, was a more systematic presentation of church polity than was the work of the Six Johns. The Church of Scotland was only being formed when they wrote, now it has become a reality. There is no fundamental difference between the two books concerning the nature of the ministry, but new matters need to be noted.

According to the Word, God has granted his church ecclesiastical power. "The Policie of the Kirk flowing from this Power, is an Order or Forme of spirituall Government, quhilk is exercisit be the Members appoyntit thereto be the Word of God: And therefore is gevin immediatly to the Office-beararis, be quhom it is exercisit to the Weile of the hole Bodie."[21]

"It is proper to Kings . . . to be callit Lordis . . . over their Subjectis . . . bot it is proper to Christ onlie to be callit Lord and Master in the Spirituall Government of the Kirk, and all uthers that beiris Office therein, aucht not to usurp Dominion therein, nor be callit Lordis, bot onlie Ministeris, Disciples, and Servantis. For it is Christis proper Office to command and rewl his Kirk universall, and every particular Kirk, throw his Spirit and Word, be the Ministrie of Men."[22]

"So in the Policie of the Kirk sum are appointit to be Rewlaris, and the rest of the Members thereof to be rewlit, and obey according to the Word of God, and Inspiratioun of his Spirit, alwayis under one Heid and chiefe Governour, Jesus Christ."[23]

The polity of the church consists of Doctrine (including the administration of the Sacraments), Discipline, and Distribution. To fulfill these functions there are three sorts of office-bearers: preachers, elders, and deacons. "3. And all these may be callit be ane generall Word, Ministers of the Kirk. For albeit the Kirk of God be rewlit and governit be Jesus Christ, who is the onlie King, hie Priest, and Heid thereof, yit he useis the Ministry of Men, as the most necessar Middis for this purpose. . . . 4. And to take away all Occasion of Tyrannie, he willis that they sould rewl with mutuall Consent of Brether, and Equality of Power, every one according to thair Functiones."[24]

The offices of pastor, elder, and deacon ought to continue perpetually in the Kirk, being necessary for the government and policy of the same.

Ambitious titles invented in "the Kingdome of Antichrist," together with the offices dependent thereon, ought utterly to be rejected.

Chapter four, "Of the Office-beararis in particular, and first of the Pastoris or Ministeris," is the grandfather of American Presbyterian descriptions of the nature and work of the minister.

"1. Pastors, Bischops, or Ministers, ar they wha are appointit to particular Congregationes, quhilk they rewll be the Word of God, and over the quhilk they watch." [Follow the titles by which the minister is described.]

2. A minister must have a certain flock assigned to him, to which he is elected by the people.

3. No man may become a minister without a lawful call.

4. Those who are called by God, and elected by a church whose call they accept, may not leave their posts.

5. Only by license of Presbytery or Assembly may a man leave.

"6. Unto the Pastors apperteinis Teaching of the Word of God, in

Season and out of Season, publicklie and privatelie, alwayes travelling to edifie and discharge his Conscience, as Gods Word prescryves to him."[25]

"7. Unto the Pastors onlie apperteins the Administration of the Sacramentis, in lyke Manner as the Administration of the Word: for baith ar appointit be God as Meanes to teach us, the ane be the Ear, and the uther be the Eyes and uther Senses, that be baith Knawledge may be transferrit to the Mynde.

"8. It apperteinis be the same Reason to the Pastors to pray for the People, and namely for the Flock committed to his Charge, and to blesse them in the Name of the Lord, who will not suffer the Blessings of his faithfull Servants to be frustrat."[26]

The next sections urge the minister to watch over his people carefully, suiting his messages to their spiritual needs. After lawful proceedings by the Session in cases of discipline, the minister (in its name) pronounces the sentence of binding and loosing, and makes such public denunciations as are necessary. "For he is as a Messenger and Herauld betwix God and the People in all these Affairs."[27] Likewise, the minister solemnizes marriages.

In agreement with Calvin, the Second Book of Discipline also sees the office of Doctor or Teacher as a permanent office. The other forms of the ministry, ruling elders and deacons, are dealt with in remarkably modern terms. What we now call the rotation system was recommended for optional use (VI.2), though office is for life. In cities, several churches could have a common eldership.

Scotland followed Geneva in its view of the minister. Its particular statements were wrought out nearly four hundred years ago, under an unfriendly monarchy, and under a system wherein the land was largely governed by great lords, who were as influential in the church as in the state. Yet the basic principles they set forth are remarkably appropriate today. They are rooted and grounded in Scripture, insofar as is possible. They show a deep understanding of human nature, which while it changes on the surface with the changing historical circumstances is yet the same at the deeper levels. Scottish Presbyterians believed in the equality or parity of ministers. Priority of dignity was given to the preacher of the Word, but there was no hierarchy.

The Second Book of Discipline made provision for superintendents. The Church of Scotland did not believe the bishop to be a superior order of ministry, nor did it believe in ordination by a line of such hierarchical bishops. It considered each parish pastor a bishop. In the crisis of 1578 it believed that the best way to meet the needs of the time was to set apart some men as superintendents, to do some of the work that naturally falls upon diocesan bishops. The superintendent, however, was to remain a pastor. The experiment did not last long, for reasons still debated.

Early Scottish Theologians

Almost without exception, the early Scottish theologians were in agreement with the principles listed above. Some of their work was molded in the heat of controversy, but their line was that of Calvin and Knox. Having broken definitely with Rome, the Scottish theologians soon had to define and refine their concepts in the light of the Church of England on the right and the Independents on the left. Some things were perfectly clear to these men.

First, the ministry is not a human invention but a Divine gift. George Gillespie in his famous *CXI Propositions* (1647) wrote:

"I. As our Lord Jesus Christ doth invisibly teach and governe his Church by the Holy Spirit: so in gathering, preserving, instructing, building and saving thereof, he useth Ministers as his instruments, and hath appointed an order of some to teach, and others to learne in the Church, and that some should be the Flock, and others the Pastours.

"II. For beside these first founders of the Church of Christ extraordinarily sent . . , he appointed also ordinary Pastors and Teachers, for the executing of the Ministery, even untill his coming againe unto Judgement, Eph. 4:11, 12, 13. Wherefore, also as many as are of the number of Gods People, or will bee accounted Christians, ought to receive and obey the ordinary Ministers of Gods Word and Sacraments, (lawfully though mediately called) as the Stewards and Ambassadours of Christ himself."

The Provincial Assembly of London, 1654, wrote in defense of Presbyterianism against the Anglican claims. This group also had a lofty view of the ministry. Its first proposition was, "That the Office of Ministry of the Word and Sacraments is necessary in the Church by Divine Institution."[28] Furthermore, ". . . The Ecclesiasticall Ministry is an Order, Function, or Office, that hath its Originall from Heaven; not from an Ordinance of Parliament, but of the Lord. . . ."[29]

Second, all the Scottish theologians were agreed upon the necessity of having only worthy men in the ministry, men of ability, lawfully called. George Gillespie's Proposition III expresses it adequately for all:

"It is not lawfull for any man how fit soever and how much soever inriched or beautified with excellent gifts, to undertake the Administration either of the Word or Sacraments by the will of private persons, or others who have not power and right to Call; much lesse is it lawfull by their owne judgement or arbitrement, to assume and arrogate the same to themselves: But before it bee lawfull to undergoe that Sacred Ministery in Churches constituted, a Special Calling, yea beside, a lawfull Election (which alone is not sufficient) a mission, or sending, or . . . Ordination, is necessarily required, and that both for the avoiding of confusion, and to bar out or shut the door (so far as in us lieth) upon impostors; as also by reason of divine institution delivered to us in the Holy Scripture. (Ro. 10:15, Heb. 5:4; Titus 1:5; I Tim. 1:14.)"[30]

The General Assembly, as a scanning of its *Acts* reveals, year after year made evident its concern for a worthy ministry. In 1642, for instance, it declared that presbyteries and synods "should proceed diligently in processe against all persons that shall reproach or scandall ministers, with the censures of the Kirk, even to the highest. . . ."[31] While demanding that laymen should respect their ministers, the Assembly was even more determined that ministers should be men worthy of respect. The Assembly of 1646 warned against corrupt life, slighting of family worship, tippling, minced oaths, speaking ill of the godly, thinking the Sabbath ends with the sermon, and being unconversant with the Scripture. In their calling as ministers, they were not to be corrupt in such respects as manner of entrance into the ministry, silence in the public cause, idleness, want of zeal, and lifelessness in preaching. While some of the actions of the Assembly seem rather legalistic, the Assembly of 1646 struck a profound and permanently valid note, "The first and main sin, reaching both to our personall carriage and callings, we judge to be, not studying how to keep communion and fellowship with God in Christ, but walking in a naturall

way, without imploying of Christ or drawing vertue from him, to in-
able us unto sanctification, and preaching in spirit and power."[32]

Third, the Scottish theologians were certain of the validity of their
ministry. Their men were duly called of God and by the church to particular tasks, were properly examined by ministers, and were ordained
with prayer and the laying on of hands of other ministers (presbyters). Against the Anglicans they consistently contended that there is
but one order of ministry, and that the presbyterate. The Scots did not
deny the right of bishops to ordain, for a bishop is a presbyter, and all
presbyters have that right! The London Presbyterians were equally as
insistent upon the validity of Presbyterian orders. They insisted "That
a Bishop and Presbyter are all one [in Scripture]; and that Ordination by Presbyters is most agreeable [to the Scripture pattern]."[33]

Fourth, just as none may take upon him the office of the minister
without a call, so "none may do the Work of the Ministry without
Ordination."[34] Presbyterians recognized that extraordinary cases
might arise, but wisely they said, "Though we will not prescribe
against necessity, yet we would not have necessity pretended where
none is."[35] At the 1640 Assembly in Scotland, there was heated discussion over the lay religious meetings among the Irish Presbyterians,
whose ministers had been driven away. Rutherford, Dickinson, Liv-
ingston, and Blair argued that under the circumstances these lay meetings were acceptable. Bishop Guthrie disagreed. The discussion
ultimately was based on the need of order in the church. In the Scottish church, probationers preached, with the approval of presbytery,
for the trial of their gifts. Samuel Rutherford insisted that ordination
is not magic. "Ordination of pastors is not that of absolute *necessity*,
but in an exigence (of necessity) the election of the people or some
other thing may supply the *want* of it."[36] Gillespie agreed. "I hold the
laying on of hands to be no sacrament, nor efficacious and operative
for the giving of the Holy Ghost."[37] The Scots did not hold to a sacra-
mental concept of ordination, but they did take it seriously and they
considered ordination normally to be essential. "Ordination is necessary and essential to the calling of a minister . . . Shall the visible political church of Christ, which is the purest and most perfect republic
in the world, have less order and more confusion in it than a civil republic? Ambassadors, commissioners, officers of state, judges, gen-

erals, admirals, with the subordinate commanders in armies and navies, do not run unsent, nor act without power, authority and commission given them."[38]

In the fifth place, Calvinist ministers have always been ordained to the ministry of the church universal—to "the gospel ministry." This point of view was made clear in the seventeenth-century debates with those Separatist sects which declared that "a minister as oft as he changeth his place and people needed a new ordination." Thus the authors of *Jus Divinum Ministerii Evangelici* insisted that "A Minister is a Minister of the Church Catholick visible."[39] Samuel Rutherford, Matthew Poole, and other Scottish leaders were in complete agreement. By the middle of the seventeenth century the Congregationalists were agreeing with the Presbyterians that the man who is ordained as a pastor is ordained to the Church Catholic, not simply as pastor of a local church. Thomas Torrance speaks for the Church of Scotland today: "In the Church of Scotland we ordain a man to the ministry of the Word and Sacraments in the Church of God, because we believe it is Christ Himself who ordains." Professor Torrance goes on to show that the minister is of course under the discipline of the Church of Scotland, and that he must respect the polity of churches which do not accept Presbyterian orders. "It claims that its careful and orderly transmission of ordination from generation to generation is in full conformity to the apostolic ordinances and teaching."[40]

OF INDEPENDENCY

For nearly two hundred years Presbyterianism was the strongest rival of Anglicanism. Both were state religions, national churches, and both had a high view of the role and function of the ministry, as well as a noble concept of worship. Despite differences in church government, in many respects they were alike. Even the Covenanters were Royalists to the last.

But in England as well as on the Continent, the sects began to complicate matters. Both Luther and Calvin had some serious reservations about the sects. Current research has made it clear that caution should be exercised in discussing these sects, whether those of the Continent or those of the British Isles. Generalizations are dangerous. That Calvin and Luther had grounds for their fears concerning the sects is true of some, at least, but it is not true of all. Genuine Christians, highly intelligent and deeply devoted, could be found among the sects as well as in the main-line churches. Only an expert is able to describe in detail the various sects in the British Isles.[41] For our purposes, we can simply call all of them the Independents.

The English Presbyterians were willing to "tarry for the magistrate," that is, to seek reform by legal means, but there came along another group who were not willing "to tarrie for anie." Beginning about 1567, Separatist churches were founded. On grounds of conscience the Separatists defied both the Established Church and the State. A Separatist leader, Robert Browne, believed in a "gathered church," rather than a national church, one consisting of those gathered out of the world by God. The Separatist or Independent groups considered the Episcopalians and the Presbyterians alike to be too hierarchical. In polity the sects were congregational. Henry Barrowe stressed the democratic aspect of church government. In general, the sects saw no scriptural grounds for the distinction between laity and clergy, for all believers are priests. Anyone who desires may preach if the Spirit urges him to do so. (Naturally the Presbyterians and Episcopalians considered this a dangerous philosophy.) Sacraments are not essential, and any Christian can administer them. Complete democracy is the supreme key to church government (and so in time to all government, though this was not yet clear). There is no human authority over the local congregation, which can ordain anyone it pleases. The whole power of God, ecclesiastically speaking, lies in the congregation, which can install or eject a minister at will, "for good cause." Ministers are definitely subordinate to the local church.

The English Baptists, some of whose roots were in Independency, some in continental Anabaptism, became one of the strongest sects. Interestingly, some of the earlier English Baptists did not practice immersion.

The Independents, whether Baptists or not, were firm advocates of religious freedom. They upheld the supremacy of conscience over the laws of the state, of king, of parliament, or of Pope. As a rising force in Cromwell's armies, they helped to behead King Charles I, and they gave a legalistic twist to Protestant ethics that is still with us. The

English-speaking race is greatly indebted to the Independents for their emphasis on freedom of conscience and on religious toleration, as well as for their rich contributions to the New World. We likewise owe to some of the Independents two unfortunate concepts: (1) that God's will is to level everybody down to one plane, for equality is the first law of man; (2) that because fixed liturgy and ceremonial have been misused by some, they should be abolished and every minister ought to be his own liturgist, thus preserving true worship. Both ideas are half-truths.

The typical American concept of the ministry has probably been influenced more by the Independents than by the Roman Catholics, Presbyterians, and Anglicans. This has proved to be a mixed blessing.

THE WESTMINSTER ASSEMBLY OF DIVINES

Civil war began between Charles I and the heavily Puritan Parliament. Bishops were excluded from the House of Lords, and episcopacy and the Book of Common Worship were outlawed. The Puritans sought the allegiance of the Scottish people, promising to re-order the Church of England along the best Reformed lines. The famous Westminster Assembly of Divines, summoned in July 1643, labored eight years. It was chosen by the two houses of Parliament, and numbered thirty laymen; 121 English clergymen, including half a dozen Independents, a few Episcopalians; and eight commissioners from the Church of Scotland. These Scots, six of whom attended, were influential far beyond their numbers. Out of the Assembly came the *Westminster Confession of Faith*, the *Larger* and *Shorter Westminster Catechisms*, and a *Directory of Public Worship*.

American Presbyterianism has been strongly influenced by the work of the Westminster divines. The concept of the ministry is treated in the Form of Government, with supplementary material in the Directory and in the Confession. The principles are set forth in a section entitled "Concerning the Doctrinal Part of Ordination of Ministers." Here again it is declared that no man may intrude himself into the ministry without a lawful call; ordination is always to be continued in the church, and is to be considered "the solemn setting apart of a person to some public Church office."[42] A man, to be ordained, must have a call to some particular church or other ministerial charge. The minister is to be a person duly qualified in character and in gifts. Presbytery examines him. He may not be thrust upon a congregation against its will. Several paragraphs call for comment.

"5. The power of ordering the whole work of ordination is in the whole presbytery . . ." including the elders. Ordination should be held in a designated place within the bounds of presbytery.

"10. Preaching presbyters orderly associated, either in cities or neighboring villages, are those to whom the imposition of hands doth appertain, for those congregations within their bounds respectively."[43]

Taken together, these two principles show that in traditional Presbyterianism the whole presbytery orders the ordination, after examination, but only the ministers of Word and Sacrament impose hands upon the kneeling ordinand. In some major Presbyterian bodies today, ruling elders also lay hands upon the ordinand.

"11. In extraordinary cases, something extraordinary may be done, until a settled order may be had, yet keeping as near as possibly may be to the rule."[44] This sound principle still prevails. In the next sentence, the Assembly said that an extraordinary situation existed at that time. In dealing with extraordinary situations, the Assembly said: ". . . and yet notwithstanding, it is requisite that ministers be ordained for them by some, who, being set apart themselves for the work of the ministry, have power to join in the setting apart others, who are found fit and worthy. . . ." The suggestion is then made that some godly ministers of London may associate for the purposes of ordaining ministers for the city and vicinity and for the military chaplaincy, "keeping as near to the ordinary rules forementioned as possibly they may."[45]

Section 13 gives an interesting reminder of the medieval custom of purchasing benefices, for it warns that no money or gift of any sort may be received by any of the presbytery, from the person about to be ordained, or on his behalf.[46]

Most of the practices in the Directory which relate to the ministry are still in our current directories. Of particular interest are a few sentences. The candidate is to be carefully examined, ". . . touching the evidences of his calling to the holy ministry; and, in particular, his fair and direct calling to that place."[47] Significantly, "(7) The proportion of his gifts in relation to the place unto which he is called shall be considered."[48] Many a tragic situation could have been avoided by following this principle. . . . The candidate is to show his ability to render a portion of either Testament into Latin.[49] Ordination as a presbyter in the Church of England is valid, though the candidate should be examined carefully.

Certain passages in the Confession also have relevance to the authority of the minister. The functions of the minister are indicated (XXI.v). "Unto this Catholick Visible Church, Christ hath given the Ministry, Oracles, and Ordinances of God, for the gathering and perfecting of the Saints in this Life to the End of the World. . . ." (XXV.iii). The two sacraments may be dispensed only by a minister of the Word lawfully ordained (XXVII.iv).

Chapter XXX, which deals with Church Censures, says that the Lord Jesus, as Head of the Church, "hath therein appointed a Government in the Hand of Church Officers, distinct from the Civil Magistrate" (XXX.ii). "To these Officers the Keys of the Kingdom of Heaven are committed, by Virtue whereof they have Power respectively to retain and remit Sins; to shut that Kingdom against the Impenitent, both by the Word and Censures; and to open it unto penitent Sinners by the Ministry of the Gospel, and by Absolution from Censures, as Occasion shall require" (XXX.ii).[50]

Church government, according to the Westminster divines, lies in the church officers rather than in the congregation directly. This is Presbyterianism, not Congregationalism. This is representative democracy, and also freedom of the church from the civil magistrate. Further, the power of the keys is vested in the church officers, not in the people as a whole.

The Westminster Standards emphasize the fact that the Word of God is presented to men through the ministry of the Word. In the Larger Catechism we read: "The Word of God is to be preached only by such as are sufficiently gifted, and also duly approved and called to that Office."[51] "They that are called to labour in the Ministry of the Word, are to preach sound Doctrine diligently, in Season and out of Season; plainly, not in the enticing Words of Man's Wisdom, but in Demonstration of the Spirit, and of Power; faithfully, making known the whole Counsel of God; wisely, applying themselves to the Necessities and Capacities of the Hearers; zealously, with fervent love to God and the Souls of his People; sincerely, aiming at his Glory, and their Conversion, Edification, and Salvation."[52]

In the Directory of Worship there is a section on Public Reading of the Holy Scriptures. Not all are to be permitted to read publicly, but only "Pastors and Teachers" and occasionally "such as intend the ministry."[53] Thomas Leishman notes that so far as public reading of the Scriptures is concerned, the English Presbyterians carried the day against the Scots, who for years had used lay readers. Nine of thirteen readers reported to the Synod of Fife in 1627 were holders of the M.A. degree![54]

"Where there are more Ministers in a Congregation than one, and they of different gifts, each may more especially apply himself to Doctrine or Exhortation, according to the gift wherein he most excelleth, and as they shall agree between themselves."[55] Here is a charter for a team ministry such as is becoming popular today. These words envision one gifted in preaching, the other in teaching. Gifts of pastoral care might also have been listed. Consultations—staff conferences and job descriptions—are implied.

There is a lengthy section in the Directory "Concerning Visitation of the Sick," which shows considerable pastoral zeal, albeit not much understanding of psychology. "It is the duty of the Minister not only to teach the people committed to his charge in public, but privately; and particularly to admonish, exhort, reprove, and comfort them, upon all seasonable occasions, so far as his time, strength, and personal safety will permit.

"He is to admonish them, in time of health, to prepare for death; and, for that purpose, they are often to confer with their Minister about the estate of their souls; and, in times of sickness, to desire his advice and help, timely and seasonably, before their strength and understanding fail them."[56] The paragraphs that follow discuss a pastoral ministry to the sick in terms deeply Christian, and, paradoxically, strangely modern and naïvely medieval. Following prayer, the minister should advise the sick man to set his house in order, pay his debts, make restitution, be reconciled, fully forgive. . . . The pastor here pictured is no mere hired hand!

BAXTER ON THE REFORMED PASTOR

The turbulent years of the sixteenth and seventeenth centuries in Britain were filled with ecclesiastical controversies. There were many unworthy men in the ministry, but there were also many godly and gifted men who served God. Richard Baxter represents Puritanism at its best. He was a moderate Puritan who strove for harmony between Presbyterians, Independents, and Episcopalians. Himself episcopally ordained, and once offered a bishopric, he could not accede to the law of 1662 in which episcopal ordination was declared essential for the Christian ministry. With 1800 other ministers he became a Nonconformist.[57] Richard Baxter was a scholar, of broad cultural interests, but above all he was a great pastor. Hugh Martin has skillfully edited a condensation of Baxter's classic, *The Reformed Pastor*, written in 1655. The title refers not to the Presbyterian minister but to the minister "recalled to faithful service," no matter what his ecclesiastical party. One of Baxter's sentences is often quoted: "If God would but reform the ministry, and set them on their duties zealously and faithfully, the People would certainly be reformed. All Churches either rise or fall as the ministry doth rise or fall (not in riches or worldly grandeur) but in knowledge, zeal and ability for their work."[58]

Ministers would profit by periodically reading *The Reformed Pastor* for the refreshing of their souls. Thus, "We must so teach others as to be ready to learn of any that can teach us . . ."[59] And, "God that thrust out a proud angel will not entertain there a proud preacher. Methinks we should remember at least the title of a *Minister*. It is this pride at the root that feedeth all the rest of our sins."[60] The pastor would do well to lend Baxter to some of his laymen. "Entertain not any unworthy thoughts of your pastors, because we here confess our own sins. You know it is men and not angels that are put by God in the office of church guides; and you know that we are imperfect men. . . . And therefore see that you love and imitate the holiness of your pastors, but take not occasion of disesteeming or reproaching them for their infirmities. . . ."[61]

VI

CHANGING CONCEPTS
OF THE MINISTRY IN AMERICA

The early settlers in America were indeed a mixed lot. At first they came mostly from the lower walks of life. Many were seeking religious freedom, but others were seeking to escape from a bad economic or social situation at home. Some came for political freedom.

The colonists brought to America all the Old World traditions, but some of them were dissatisfied with those traditions. To be in the New World meant to establish new ways. Old traditions had to be modified. Though some were rigid and unchanging in their determination to cling to the old ways, the majority were more flexible and learned to adapt to a new land and to achieve new attitudes. Changes did not come overnight. It was a hundred years before the changed attitudes really pervaded the whole of ecclesiastical life and thought. There were times when the revolutionary spirit probably went too far and cast aside some things of permanent value.

SIGNIFICANT CHANGES

One change is of great importance. In Europe there was a relationship between church and state which proved to be impossible to maintain in America. In "the Old Country" there were national churches; in the New World they became denominations. Thus the Presbyterian was the National Church of Scotland, while the Episcopal was the National Church of England. In America, there were no true state churches, though several of the new colonies were set up with religious establishments. After the Revolutionary War, the state constitutions declared for the separation of church and state. The early colonists were members of or related to the major churches, but the sect type of churches gained rapidly in influence in the New World. The Anglican church failed to give the new colonies a bishop, and left them subject to the bishop of London. This meant that men had to go to London to be ordained by the bishop. It also meant that American Episcopalians could not have their children confirmed. Had the Episcopalians been wiser, and given each colony a bishop, they might have won America. The rough and ready men on the frontier did not like the arrangement which kept the chief religious privileges in London. On the other hand, the Virginia situation was such that the vestrymen controlled the minister, and so long as there was no bishop there could be no life-tenure pastorates by Episcopal clergymen. This points to a second basic fact about the religious atmosphere in the New World.

There was a far greater emphasis on the laity, almost from the beginning. Laymen in America were less dependent upon ministers, and they took into their own hands many things which had been left to the minister in the old country. Rarely did laymen administer the sacraments, but they conducted public worship, read the Word of God, read sermons by well-known divines, and perhaps a few preached their own sermons. In the religious life of most of the colonies, laymen were notably prominent.

A third element was extreme individualism. American colonial life was rough and crude, isolated and often dangerous. There were communities established without a church. Without a regular church or regular ministry, thousands of folk who had been nominal church members back home soon became indifferent to religion, especially in institutional form. Frontier life tends to be not only rough but also fundamentally self-centered. Man depends on his own efforts, and he dies unless he does so. But while it is good to stay alive, one can lose his own soul in the process. Many in the New World were so busy taking care of themselves that they forgot God. It is good for human beings to trust in their own abilities, but American life went too far in this direction, and this led to an excessive individualism. Some of the folk who came to the New World were already infected with the virus of individualism. Such sects as the Levellers, the Dunkards, and the Seekers were arch exponents of individualism, and the Baptists were not far behind.

No one who has seen the beautiful old estates along the James

River in Virginia can possibly believe that all our colonial ancestors
were uncultured. Every colony had some families of fine culture and
advanced education. Naturally much of the leadership of the new
colonies came from the educated group. America as a whole, however, was not settled by the upper levels of European society, but
mainly by folk from the lower classes, with a large sprinkling of
people from the rising middle class. In this New World, true democracy began to flourish as it had never flourished in the old.

A fourth major point of change was in the emphasis on religious
freedom. The Puritans came to this country to be free to worship God
in their own way. Practically, they denied this freedom of worship to
others for many years. It was the insistence of men like Roger Williams and Samuel Davies that finally led to the genuine acceptance of
the concept of religious freedom for all men. The belief that all men
have a right to worship God as they please, and that no state can force
worship upon its citizens, became enshrined in our Constitution. It is
part of our way of life. This had a vital effect upon the ministry. The
inevitable outcome of such religious freedom was a multiplicity of
sects. The colonists came from all of western Europe, though notably
from the British Isles. The French Huguenots and the Dutch Calvinists
made their contributions, along with the German Lutherans and the
various pietistic sects. The Christian world had not known such a vast
conglomeration of denominations. Their proliferation has by the
twentieth century become a scandal.

It is significant also that the churches in America developed from
local church organizations before they set up wider administrative
groups such as presbyteries, consociations, or dioceses. Even in the old
line churches which had the tradition of a national church, the tendency was to stress the importance of the local church. Localism
historically came first in this country, then later a loyalty to the larger
concept of the church. Even to this day the denominations with regional, state, and national courts or councils find a certain lack of
loyalty and an overemphasis upon the work of the local church. Many
ministers treat all too lightly their responsibility to the larger church.
And laymen of all denominations tend to think first of their own local
program. "If we have anything left, we can give it to our denominational program, but our first responsibility is to our own church," is

the theme song of multitudes of modern American deacons. In Scotland, the national church became Presbyterian and then Presbyterianism gradually seeped down into the parishes. In Europe, countries were likely to follow the religion of the princes! But localism was a fundamental characteristic of the American scene. Only in America has the congregational form of church government (pure democracy) really taken hold. Witness the Baptists!

The American scene, then, made its rich contribution to the concept of the ministry, through setting up a wall between church and state, and ruling out "establishment of religion"; through giving the laity far more importance in church leadership; through stressing religious freedom with its consequent sectarianism; and through localism or congregationalism.

We do not know what would have happened if with each new batch of colonists there had come an able and devoted minister. Some wonderful men did come to the New World with their people, but far too few. Neither the quantity nor the quality of ministers in the colonies was good enough to maintain the ministry at a high level. The people of the New World often suffered from an inadequate ministry, whether from Europe or from this new land.

MINISTERS IN THE COLONIAL ERA

The shortage of ministers meant that for years certain communities had to do without the Lord's Supper. The Pilgrims landed in 1620 without an ordained minister. Elder Brewster gave spiritual leadership, but he did not administer the sacraments. The colonists were without the sacraments for four years before their first minister, John Lyford, came. The Dutch colonists went for two years in New Amsterdam without the sacraments. Manifestly the colonists believed that the sacraments were to be administered only by ordained men.

When ministers did arrive they were held in such high esteem that it was not good for their souls. No group of ministers has ever had more real power than the first Puritan ministers in this country. "Between 1630 and 1641 sixty-five ministers arrived in Massachusetts. Because of the belief held by their flocks that they were divinely inspired, great deference was given their views and judgments, tending to make them opinionated and determined to have their own way."[1] Suffrage was limited to church members, and this gave the clergy great power over the political life. Though unofficial, the influence of the clergy was strong.

Not all of the clergy received adulation. The first clergyman of the Pilgrims, John Lyford, was soon expelled for treason. An early Swedish minister, according to two Dutch ministers writing in 1657, was "a man of impious and scandalous habits, a wild drunken, unmannerly clown, more inclined to look into the wine can than into the Bible. . . ."[2] A number of early German ministers were weak and quarrelsome. Some of the Episcopal ministers in the South were second-rate men.[3] Colonial Presbyterians also had their share of weak ministers. Every major religious group, apparently, had a few grossly weak men, and others who were mediocre, along with a few men of rare ability and noble spirit.

From the records, it would seem that proportionately there were far more morally weak ministers in the colonial church than is the case today. For instance, Professor Trinterud has shown that the ministers of the Old Side group of Presbyterians were less admirable morally than they were ecclesiastically. "The supreme tragedy of the Old Side was the moral failure of its clergy." Of the twelve men who forced the schism in 1741, four had unworthy records prior to 1741, four more were found guilty of serious offenses, and two of the first four sank deeper.[4] Not all of the small number of New Side ministers would pass muster today.[5] The Reverend David Rice, pioneer Presbyterian missionary to Kentucky, who established churches at Danville and Harrodsburg, asserted that some of the clergymen in Kentucky ". . . did not appear to possess much of the spirit of the Gospel."[6] An inspection of the records by Robert Davidson showed ". . . that nearly half the entire number of preachers were, at one time or other, subjected to church censures more or less severe; several being cut off for heresy or schism, two deposed for intemperance, one suspended for licentiousness, several rebuked for wrangling, and others for other improprieties unbecoming the gravity or dignity of the clerical character. . . . This is a development fraught with solemn instruction, warning the Church that instead of sending to new and promising settlements her weakest men, as if anything were good enough for such stations, it would be far wiser to send the most efficient laborers, picked men, who would leave the impress of their own commanding virtues upon succeeding generations."[7]

Whisky was served at all kinds of functions, and often the clergy would be paid in whisky. Dr. W. W. Sweet's comment on the Presbyterians is applicable to other denominations and other sections in the early years. "And with a part of their salary quite commonly paid in whisky it will not be surprising to learn that the most frequent cause for the discipline of ministers by the presbyteries was their too copious use of ardent spirits."[8] Ministers as well as laymen sometimes were found guilty of adultery.

Judgmentally, if the early ministers had been as morally sound as we expect ministers to be today, perhaps the church would have had a greater impact on early American life, and perhaps the office of the ministry would have been more universally respected. But theirs was a wilder era and in some ways the temptations were greater. In America, unlike certain other parts of the world, the office of minister does not automatically give a man the respect of those around him. He receives the respect of his people only when he deserves it, and not because of his office. Ralph C. Deal in 1906 commented that whereas in earlier years deference was automatically paid to a minister, no longer does he receive it unless he deserves it. ". . . it is the *man* that is commanding the respect and not simply the office."[9]

Our Reformed ancestors would have said that the office of minister in itself deserves respect, and that any man who holds that office should be given respect until he proves himself unworthy of it. And they were right. Their constant effort to examine with genuine care every candidate for the ministry meant that they wanted to be very sure that no one was ordained to the ministry who was insincere, immoral, or heretical. Respect is vastly different from obsequious adulation. Too strong an emphasis on "the man, not the office," may be just another form of salvation by works. The late James H. Taylor, who for many years was pastor of the Central Presbyterian Church of Washington, related an incident which speaks to our need. On one occasion at a party in Washington, Dr. Taylor met the new and distinguished British Ambassador. "It is an honor," said Taylor, "to meet the ambassador of so great a king." Replied the ambassador, "Ah, sir, but you are an ambassador of the King of kings."

Although the colonial church desired worthy and able clergymen, it was not easy to obtain qualified ministers. Few good men would come from Europe, and there were very few institutions for ministerial training in the colonies. The Anglicans had to send men back to England for ordination, while the German Reformed could ordain a man only upon permission from the homeland. Under these conditions, some groups began to ordain their own ministers. The German Reformed Church in America insisted that John Philip Boehm become a minister. He was a schoolmaster-farmer, the son of a Reformed minister. Soon after he arrived in the Perkiomen Valley, he was asked to lead religious services. After five years he permitted himself to become a minister and to assume the full duties of a clergyman, including the administration of the sacraments. Two years later a regular minister arrived. Boehm was denounced as a mere farmer. He went to New York to consult the Dutch Reformed ministers there. They urged him to consult the Classis in Amsterdam. The Classis gave an answer which was in the true Reformed tradition. Under the circumstances the action of Boehm in assuming ministerial functions was justified, but he should now seek to be properly ordained. To this suggestion he gladly agreed, and he was ordained by the Dutch ministers in New York.[10]

INFLUENCE OF THE REVIVALS

The religious revivals that swept across America following 1730 and again around 1800-1830 did much to democratize the concept of the ministry, stressing the personal character of the minister. The first great American revival was really threefold, and has been called, "The Great Awakening." In the Middle Atlantic States the Presbyterians were led by the Tennents, chief of whom was Gilbert. The Tennent group had been trained by William Tennent in his famous Log College at Neshaminy, Pennsylvania. Soon they were aided by some men who had been trained in New England. The revivalistic tendencies of the Tennents were opposed by what came to be known as the Old Side Presbyterians, all of whom had been trained on the continent. Leonard Trinterud has given a detailed account of this first great Presbyterian split, in his excellent book, *The Forming of an American Tradition*. Nominally it centered around questions of creedal subscription, a degree from a European university, and "higher educational standards." Trinterud demonstrates that the Old Side was trying to bring over to this country Old World patterns which were not suitable. He thinks the New Side men were as well educated as the Old, and were as loyal to the creed, though perhaps less legalistic about it. Morally and spiritually, believes Trinterud, the New Side group were superior to the Old Side. Old Side was cold, correct, and dogmatic; New Side was warm, evangelical, and equally orthodox. Old Side was not evangelistic in spirit, New Side was. While the New Side ordained men without European degrees, they would not ordain uneducated or weak men. The Old Side was particularly zealous to have every minister subscribe to the Confession of Faith.

At the Synod of 1734, Gilbert Tennent submitted an overture proposing that presbyteries begin to take seriously the requirements for ordination set forth in the Westminster Standards, not only as to education but also as to experimental religion. "The synod [1734] thereupon passed two overtures, one urging that great care be taken in admitting men to the ministry, and a second ordering that all ministers were to be most diligent and faithful in their duties."[11] Strong arguments took place over certain individuals whom one side or the other deemed unfit or ill prepared for the ministry. Personal dislikes, jealousy, and other low motives were not completely missing from the arguments. Both sides wanted good men, but they differed as to what this meant. Did "well-trained" necessitate a European degree? And was a religious experience of salvation necessary for a preacher? The Tennents never said that there was but one valid kind of religious experience, although they did feel strongly that some of the Old Side ministers were intellectually orthodox but lacked a genuine conversion experience. "The Danger of an Unconverted Ministry," Gilbert Tennent's famous sermon, was so intemperately stated as to arouse much bitterness. Later he confessed that in the heat of the conflict he had gone too far.

Despite their high standards, the Old Side men were too lax in disciplining erring ministers. The New Side had fewer men guilty of drunkenness and immorality, possibly because their discipline was firmer. Out of these trying years of conflict, the Calvin-Knox principles emerged in American Presbyterianism. Each candidate was to be examined with great care by the presbytery, though at the beginning examination was by the synod. No man could be ordained *sine titulo* (without a call to a particular church) except missionaries to the frontier. Presbytery had the final say concerning the acceptance of a call. Ordination was by the preaching elders.

By the 1770's a college education was within the reach of any prospective student, who could be aided by church funds if necessary. Presbyteries became reluctant to ordain men who had only an academy education. Jacob Green, a Harvard graduate, warned in 1775 that the Presbyterian system of educated ministers was too tough, and that, needing 300 ministers, the Presbyterians should seek schoolteachers who could double as ministers. The proposal failed. "The ideal of a highly trained clergy, the fear of heresy born of ignorance, and an intense dislike of shoddy preaching led the synod to strive constantly for higher standards."[12] "Reason tells us," wrote James Finley, "that he who is to teach others, should not himself be a Novice . . ."[13] In 1785 the synod by a great majority responded in the negative to an overture: "Whether in the present state of the church in America, and the scarcity of ministers to fill our numerous congregations, the Synod, or Presbyteries, ought therefore to relax, in any degree, in the literary qualifications required of entrants into the ministry?"[14] This answer was to characterize Presbyterianism through the years. At the time of the Revolution, Presbyterians were the second strongest church in the nation. In the next forty years priority in numbers was lost to the Baptists and Methodists, whose ministerial standards were much lower. Many Presbyterian scholars today think that in the circumstances our ancestors were wrong to hold to their high educational standards. Other scholars think our ancestors were right. Someone had to educate the American people, and someone had to hold forth a gospel that would challenge the upper third of society. These two things the Presbyterians did exceedingly well.

The Great Awakening in New England 1734-1760 was led by the mighty Jonathan Edwards, perhaps the greatest American theologian. Edwards and the powerful preacher George Whitefield were leaders of the awakening along the Atlantic seaboard. At times the behavior at the revival services was boisterous and unwholesome. In 1743 the General Convention of Congregational Ministers in Massachusetts, in their *Testimony* against certain doctrinal and practical disorders, asserted that in practice uneducated persons without any regular call were "taking upon themselves to be preachers of the word of God," that men were being ordained without a particular call; that ministers were itinerating and invading the parishes of regular pastors, sometimes judging those pastors too harshly.[15]

Despite these weaknesses, and doctrinal errors taught by some, there were real values in the awakening in New England. Thousands were added to the churches; old members were deepened in piety; the number of ministerial candidates increased; and the ministers themselves became more devoted.

According to W. W. Sweet, the Southern phase of the Great Awakening was both more interdenominational in character and more uncultured, bearing the stamp of the frontier. It was here that the Baptists and the Methodists became a vital force on the American scene. "In other words it marks the real beginning of the democratizing of religion in America."[16] The Southern awakening actually began among the Presbyterians, with Samuel Davies as the key figure. Davies had to persuade the Virginia authorities that the English Act of Toleration applied to the colonies before he was allowed to preach. Davies later was the first moderator of Hanover, first Southern presbytery. Few Episcopalians, with the exception of Deveraux Jarrett, contributed to the Great Awakening. Jarrett gave assistance to the Methodist lay preachers as well as doing much preaching himself.

THE PRESBYTERIAN MINISTER, CIRCA 1776

Trinterud writes: "The ministry of colonial Presbyterianism, though modeled largely on the patterns of British Presbyterianism, had been markedly influenced by factors operating in the American scene, especially the influence of the frontier and of the Great Awakening. Most of the native-born clergy were from humble lay homes. . . . Their early education was usually received in small schools conducted in the manses of their ministers."[17] From there the students usually went on to academy or college.

Ministers in some of the older and larger city parishes received adequate salaries. Not so most ministers! The Scotch-Irish were poor to begin with, and were not accustomed to paying their ministers directly. Many ministers were forced to do secular work, mainly teaching or farming. Congregations sometimes were neglected. Trinterud believes that "In spite of hardships and handicaps, some heroic ministries were carried on by the colonial clergy. Some men, it is true, clung to the idea of an aristocratic ministry, stressed the duty of their people to 'submit' to their 'authority,' arbitrarily used exclusion from the sacraments to enforce their authority and gain submission, and earned for themselves the reputation of having no true personal religious concern for their people. The greater part of the clergy proved by lives of astounding self-sacrifice, and by lives burned out before the age of forty, that they knew no higher call than that of the Gospel ministry among the frontier people."[18] The church that produced men like Francis Makemie and Samuel Davies, Gilbert Tennent and Francis Alison, Jonathan Dickinson and John Witherspoon, can thank God for its founding fathers!

"AT THE WEST"

By 1750 the Scotch-Irish had flooded western Pennsylvania and the Valley of Virginia. Thirty years later they were pouring across the Allegheny Mountains into Tennessee and Kentucky and down the Ohio Valley. Where the people went, the ministers went, but too few and too late.

Western New York and northern Ohio were being settled mainly by people from New England. In the South, the westward trek was mainly through the Cumberland Gap. David Rice was the first Presbyterian minister to cross the mountains into Kentucky (1783). Transylvania Presbytery was organized three years later. A few years thereafter came the Synod of Kentucky.

While the Methodists and Baptists were establishing many churches and allowing untrained men to preach, the Presbyterians proceeded into the West with caution. Presbyterian ministers tended to have rather limited circuits to ride. In his resident community the minister was usually also a schoolmaster, for he was probably by far the best educated person, having a college degree and special training in theology beyond that. Naturally, as people flooded the West, the temptation came to lower the standards. This the Presbyterians stead-fastly refused to do. Instead of using lay preachers, or ordaining un-trained men, the Presbyterians decided to take the long-range view and educate a ministry. To gain more ministers, they established more colleges, and early in the nineteenth century they also established what we now call theological seminaries.[19]

Professor W. W. Sweet says: "In devising adequate frontier tech-niques Presbyterianism was handicapped by the rigidity of both its creed and polity. The numerous frontier controversies and divisions were largely the result of the lack of elasticity in Presbyterianism."[20] The great revival in the Kentucky region began under a Presbyterian minister named James McGready. He was instrumental in the conver-sion of Barton Stone, who later became first a Presbyterian minister and then a founder of the Disciples of Christ. The year 1801 found the Kentucky camp meetings at their height and the emotions encouraged to run wild. Out of this revival and the large number of professions of faith came in time three schisms. The Cumberland schism was impor-tant. The Logan County (Cumberland) revival led to the influx of many converts and the founding of new churches, which in turn led to calls for more ministers. Transylvania Presbytery in the emergency authorized four men to exhort and catechize in vacant congregations. They were older, uneducated men, and the licensing brought five dis-senting votes. In 1802 Transylvania Presbytery was divided, Cumber-land Presbytery being formed from it, with ten revivalistically inclined ministers. The policy of licensing men with serious educa-tional lacks was continued by the new presbytery. The candidates were examined on experimental religion and on their motives in entering the ministry, but little was asked concerning their educational qualifi-cations. These men, despite their lack of education, seemed quite successful. In the next two years the Synod of Kentucky examined the situation and took steps to remedy it which went beyond Presbyterian law. They even abolished Cumberland Presbytery! In 1809 the Gen-eral Assembly upheld the Synod. And the Cumberland Presbyterian Church was immediately established. Using ministers with limited education, the Cumberland Church met with considerable success in the Southern mountains. Main-line Presbyterianism stuck to its guns: an educated ministry or none at all. The Cumberland Church today is steadily raising the standards of its ministry, both through its own theological seminary and through a program of in-service training for those without degrees. And the Presbyterian church leaders who state that the church was too inflexible in the Cumberland schism, continue to insist on a highly educated ministry. Looking back, we can see that some compromises might have been possible—on both sides.

No better way can be found to give the spirit of the Presbyterian ministry in the eighteenth and nineteenth centuries than to look at a few excerpts from the minutes of the Transylvania Presbytery, Kentucky.[21]

Oct. 18, 1786. Presbytery accepted the Synod's recommendation that vacant congregations should meet each Sabbath, with elders praying, selecting the Scriptures to be read, "by any proper persons whom they may appoint." To catechize vacant congregations, in accord with Synod's order, Presbytery voted, ". . . that catechists shall be appointed for the purpose of instructing the young & ignorant, but that no person shall be appointed to this office till he is first nominated by a pastor or minister of the gospel, examined & approved of by Presby.; & that he shall not by virtue of this appointment attempt to expound the Scriptures, preach the gospel or dispense the sealing ordinances thereof."

April 24, 1787. James Camper was nominated by Rev. David Rice as a catechist, "was examined on divinity & approved of."

Oct. 7, 1789. On this date Mr. James Camper, already approved as a catechist, "is permitted as a probationer for the gospel ministry to preach under the direction of Mr. Rice while he continues in the study of divinity on trial."

Oct. 4, 1792. Mr. Adam Rankin, suspended, had preached and administered the sacraments despite his suspension and was determined to go on in that way. ". . . this Pby. do unanimously declare that said Adam Rankin has no right to exercise the ministerial function at any time nor in any place & that, as he was set apart to the office of a gospel minister & the discharge of the duties of the same by the officers of the Presbyterian church, so by the same authority . . . the said office is taken from him & he forbid to discharge any of the duties of the same . . ."

Oct. 23, 1792. Speaking of the ordination of James Kemper, who had been duly examined and who had properly answered the ordination vows, ". . . then the presiding bishop, by prayer & with the laying on of the hands of the presbytery, according to the apostolic example, solemnly ordained the said James Kemper to the holy office of the gospel ministry, & was constituted the pastor of the Cincinnati and Columbia churches. The presiding minister then gave the charge to the newly ordained bishop & the people of his charge. . . ." (Note interchangeable use of bishop and minister.)

Oct. 10, 1794. "Ordered, that no congregation, or church, under the care of this pby. shall make any proposals to any minister or ministers . . . to settle amongst them as their minister . . . until he is approved by this pby. . . ."

Oct. 7-8, 1795. One John Bowman, a licentiate from Orange Presbytery, was granted permission to itinerate in Transylvania, and was commended to the vacant churches. Action was taken, after debate, ". . . that no person in the Presbyterian church shall take the liberty to exhort publicly unless he is first appointed by the Pby. . . . for that purpose."

Oct. 9, 1795. Three young men were given permission to exhort under the following limitations: "that they do not exhort oftener than once in two weeks, & not without first carefully digesting the matter of their exhortations; & they are directed not to exceed forty five minutes . . ."

Oct. 8, 1802. Two men were duly examined and licensed as probationers. Then follows the key passage. "Messrs Alexander Anderson, Finis Ewing & Sam'l King being taken under the care of pby. at our last Fall meeting as catechists & then licensed to exhort & catechise in our vacancies, & as their labors were attended with a divine blessing as pby. have reason to believe, & being universally acceptable to our vacancies, several petitions having come forward from many of our vacancies earnestly & importunately praying pby. to license them to preach the gospel,—pby. after mature deliberation considered this matter as coming under the view of that extraordinary excepted in the book of discipline, examined them on their experimental acquaintance with religion, the evidences of their call to the ministry & examined them upon their knowledge in divinity; in which trials pby. received satisfaction & licensed them to preach the gospel."

Three ministers and two ruling elders formally dissented to this licensing of Messrs. King and Ewing, both of whom had been rejected at the last meeting of presbytery as persons unfit to be continued as candidates. They stated that presbytery was put under pressure by the petitions of the people, and because the trials "consisted only in one short sermon & an examination on experimental religion & divinity, being destitute of classical learning, & they discovered no such extraordinary talents as to justify such measures." These men were later ordained by Cumberland Presbytery, along with other men of dubious educational background. The Commission of the Synod of Kentucky sent to examine them declared them unqualified.

These few excerpts from the Minutes of Transylvania Presbytery have perhaps given rather clearly the concept of the minister that prevailed in those days, as well as the tenseness of the atmosphere. It might be added that the minutes show cases of men being called up and tried before presbytery because of drunkenness, sexual misconduct, alleged heresy, alleged business chicanery, contumacy with reference to the orders of presbytery, and because of gross abuse of a Negro slave.

The Minutes of Cumberland Presbytery reveal a somewhat different atmosphere. Because of the urgent requests of the churches for ministers, men are ordained without good educational qualifications. A strong minority of Cumberland Presbytery was consistently opposed to this lowering of the standards, but the majority consistently urged "need." One minute suffices.

April 6, 1803. "Presbytery considering Robert Guthrie, Robert Houston, Matthew Hall and Samuel Hodge as persons of good standing in the church whose abilities also promise usefulness to the souls of their fellowmen, do authorize and license them to make public appointments and exercise their gifts in exhortation in any congregation or settlement within the bounds of this presbytery."[22] Note that nothing is said of the training or educational qualifications of these men.

THE AMERICAN MINISTER—BY 1860

By the early nineteenth century, American Protestantism had pretty well settled the main aspects of the question of who is a minister. The minister was seen, more clearly than in the Old World, to have a great evangelistic responsibility. He was thought of in democratic rather than in aristocratic terms. The fact that most American ministers came from poor families does not mean that they were inferior men or that they considered their calling to be anything but the highest of vocations. American ministers were aristocratic in the sense that they were a chosen, dedicated, superior group of men serving the King of kings. They were democratic in that they were from the people and of the people and for the people.

Long before the bitter Civil War, Presbyterians had made the basic decisions concerning the ministry. The line back through the Reformation concepts to the Bible is clear. No basic concepts reached by Calvin or the Scottish Reformers on this theme were abandoned. Here again are such themes as: the ministry is a gift of Christ to the church; no man may thrust himself into the ministry without a lawful call; no minister may be forced upon a church. At the operational level, these points are clear:

1. The ministry of Word and Sacrament is a practical necessity to the church, though a church may exist for a little while without a minister. This implies that ultimately the church is prior to the ministry. A few of the Scots might have had some reservations about this conclusion.

2. The ministry calls for men of noble character and deep devotion to Christ, who also are as well educated as is possible, so that they can proclaim the true, full gospel to men of all degrees of culture.

3. Their education involves a liberal arts background, philosophy and literature, the sciences and the classical languages, Greek and Latin, followed by a theological education which includes a study of the Bible with the aid of the original languages, church history, and theology.

4. The minister is subject to his brethren in presbytery.

5. He cannot itinerate except by permission of presbytery.

6. He is to be ordained by the laying on of hands of his fellow presbyters.

7. Laymen could not administer the sacraments, nor could they preach without express permission of presbytery. This was to avoid having untrained laymen ignorantly preach heresy.

Presbyterian views of the proclamation of the gospel did not change. As James H. Thornwell said in an ordination sermon preached April 30, 1836, "Oh it is a solemn thing to hear a Gospel sermon from the lips of a Gospel Minister! It is an awful thing to despise God in the person of His ambassadors! 'Take heed, therefore, how ye hear.' Hear as from God, hear as for eternity."[23]

VII

---·◇·---

WHO IS A MINISTER?

To gain self-identity is the modern minister's most difficult problem. Who am I? What does it mean to be a minister of the gospel? Is the ministry of Word and Sacrament really different from all other forms of Christian service? What is the rightful place of a Christian minister in our society? In the church? In his own thinking?

A minister of Word and Sacrament is primarily a servant of God, secondarily he is a servant of God's people, and thirdly he is a servant of mankind. The priorities are clear and important. If they are upset, the minister may indeed cease to be a true minister and become ensnared by the social mores or by his own egocentric desires.

In a general sense, every Christian is a minister. Every person who calls himself a Christian has a mission to the world, a service to render, a ministry to give. Every Christian is to testify to others by word and deed and prayer and character what it means to be a Christian. A Christian is called to serve his fellow men. Every Christian participates in the ministry that Christ is carrying out through his church in the world. It is possible, therefore, but misleading, to say that every Christian is a minister. It is far more accurate to say that every Christian has a ministry, or that every Christian participates in the ministry of the church. Christian thinkers are agreed that to be a Christian is to be a servant of God and of one's fellows, but it is misleading to say that because all Christians have a ministry, all Christians are ministers. The net result of this way of putting it is that we have denigrated the word minister. No wonder the church is having difficulty recruiting men and women for the ministry of Word and Sacrament. If everybody is a minister, why bother with ordaining some people and calling them ministers? "What is everybody's business is nobody's business."

93

One able American theologian, Arnold B. Come, has allowed himself
to be carried too far in his enthusiasm for the ministry of the laity. In
a recent book his theme is that "The church is now ready for, and its
God-given mission now demands, *the complete abandonment of the
clergy-laity distinction.* . . . The church, therefore, must shatter the
traditional image of the pastoral minister as *the* minister. . . . Until
this image of the minister is shattered, little progress will be made in
shattering the image of the laity as a group of passive, irresponsible,
second-rate Christians."[1] Dr. Come is correct in his desire to
strengthen the ministry of the laity, but the solution he suggests is
unwise.

In the New Testament the word *diakonos* (minister, servant) is
used a few times in the general sense of a ministry, but fundamentally
it is used of something distinctive rather than general. Ephesians and
the Pastoral Epistles testify to the fact that before the year A.D. 100
the church had a specialized ministry. Some men were called by God
to be ministers. They were given by the ascended Christ to the church
for its building up, "for the gathering and perfecting of the saints."[2]
All Christians have a ministry, but God has set some men apart to be
in a special and particular way pastors and teachers.

A GIFT OF GOD

In the first place, then, Reformed thinkers have always held that
the ministry is an office and a function which on the one hand is set up
by the church, but which on the other hand is given by God to the
church. And the emphasis has been on the latter. The ministry of
Word and Sacrament is not simply a device created by the church for
greater efficiency; it is actually a vital part of the church, a creation
of God. From a writer in the early nineteenth century we have this
statement: "But the pastors of the church are now, preeminently the
representatives of Christ . . . The labours of faithful pastors will be
required in all ages. The pastoral office is explicitly appointed by
Christ; by him ministers are commissioned, and in his name, in his
stead, they perform their ministerial functions. Whatever they do,
within the limits of their commission, is sanctioned by him; he con-

siders it as done by himself. They are, therefore, the most immediate and the most important representatives of Christ upon earth. . . ."[3]

More guarded are the words of the great Princeton theologian, Charles Hodge. In an address in 1855, after showing that the ministry is an office, and not simply a work (function), Hodge went on to say: "Our second remark is, that the office is of divine appointment, not merely in the sense in which the civil powers are ordained of God, but in the sense that ministers derive their authority from Christ, and not from the people. Christ has not only ordained that there shall be such officers in his Church—he has not only specified their duties and prerogatives—but he gives the requisite qualifications, and calls those thus qualified, and by that call gives them their official authority."[4] Hodge goes on to show that the church does not confer the office but does examine the candidate to determine if he be truly called, and if he is, to ordain him.

An earlier writer (1810) said, "Since, therefore, the Head of the church instituted a regular ministry in his church thousands of years ago . . . no conclusion is more safe and irrefragable than this; that a regular, standing ministry is an essential constituent of the church of God."[5]

The Scheme of Union for the Churches of South India states the matter clearly: "The uniting Churches believe that the ministry is a gift of God through Christ to His Church, which He has given for the perfecting of the life and service of all its members. . . . All . . . share in the heavenly High Priesthood of the risen and ascended Christ, from which alone the Church derives its character as a royal priesthood. . . .

"But in the Church there has at all times been a special ministry, to which men have been called by God and set apart in the Church. Those who are ordained to the ministry of the Word and Sacraments can exercise their offices only in and for the Church, through the power of Christ the one High Priest."[6]

These words echo the biblical and the Reformed view of the ministry.

The Reformed churches have consistently believed that the ministry is a gift of God to the church, though they have differed as to whether or not the ministry is essential to the church. Charles Hodge believed the ministry to be a divine institution; that it was designed to be perpetual; that it has been perpetuated; and that it was necessary to the edification and extension of the church. The ministry, he contended, is not essential in the sense that where there is no ministry there is no church. "We believe with Professor Thornwell, and with the real living church of God in all ages, that if the ministry fails, the church can make a ministry; or rather that Christ, who is in his church by the Spirit, would then, as he does now, by his divine call constitute men ministers. . . . Every vacant church is a practical proof that the ministry does not enter into the definition of the church."[7]

High church Presbyterians of Scotland in a pamphlet on *Presbyterian Orders* (1926) differed with Hodge. Christ did not endow the church "with the potentiality of evolving a ministry out of itself or of empowering or authorizing a ministry for itself. He did not give the Church power to make a ministry; He Himself made the ministry and gave it to the Church; what is given is the Ministry. . . . The original bestowal of Stewards of his Mysteries (Luke 12:42; I Cor. 4:1; Eph. 4:11), the stewards as continued, the gifts fitting men for ministry, the commission to minister—all is gift, bestowed upon the Church, not found by it out of its own inherent resources."[8] These men were in accord with the words of the Scottish General Assembly of 1698, "Ministers are sent to the people, not by the people."[9]

These two quotations, while exaggerations, state the truth that not only is the ministry a practical necessity but that as gift of God the church cannot well refuse it. If the church exists where the gospel is purely preached and heard, and the sacraments rightly administered, then surely the ministry is an essential part of the life of the church. Yet most Reformed theologians would agree with Hodge that while ministerial order is necessary, in an emergency God can give to the church a new group of ministers. If atom bombs were to wipe out all duly ordained church officers, the church would be right in praying to God to call others whom it could recognize to be his gifts to the church for a new ministry.

THE PRIESTLY FUNCTION

Ministers, in the second place, have priestly functions. The New Testament does not call ministers priests. Only Jesus Christ is called a

Priest. Yet it is true to say that the church is a priesthood and has a priestly service (1 Peter 2:4-10). That priesthood is shared by all members of the church. In a sense, every Christian is a priest. Ministers of the gospel are Christians, therefore they are priests in the sense of "the priesthood of believers." But this priesthood offers no blood sacrifices, it slaughters no lambs or oxen, no doves or pigeons, no human offspring. The New Testament priest does offer up sacrifices of praise and thanksgiving (Heb. 13:15). He offers up himself a living sacrifice (Rom. 12:1). All Christians, certainly including those set apart to be ministers, are priests in this sense. Priest is derived from presbyter, and when used by Christians today priest should not have sacrificial connotations. The Roman Church continues to put more into the word priest than should be there. Protestants often say ministers have a priestly function. They mean that the minister in his capacity as leader of worship prays for all the people rather than offering up his private devotions in public. Not all Protestant ministers understand this! When the minister prays in corporate worship he is functioning as a priest, representing all the people in offering up their desires unto God. A layman at prayer meeting may also partake of the offering up of the prayers of the people unto God, in priestly service.

Bishop Lightfoot in his great commentary on Philippians has a famous excursus on the ministry, in which he says, ". . . the minister's function is *representative* without being *vicarial*. He is a priest, as the mouthpiece, the delegate, of a priestly race. His acts are not his own, but the acts of the congregation."[10] Donald MacLeod in his Baird Lectures, 1903, agreed. "The ministry is a priesthood only in a representative capacity, appointed for the due ordering of worship and administering the sacraments. But the prophetic office [his preaching] remains in its full force; for the preaching of the Gospel . . . is emphatically the work of the ministry."[11]

In a brilliant essay, "The Priesthood of Believers," T. W. Manson points out that "the high-priestly work of Christ consists in his complete oblation of himself in obedience and love to God and in love and service of men. That work, decisively done on the Cross, is continued by Christ in the Church." He finds the focus of this high-priestly work, in which Christ and his people share, in the Eucharist. He then says: "The function of the minister who celebrates is to be the representative and spokesman of God through Christ to the congregation and of the congregation to God through Christ. As spokesman to the congregation he recalls to them the things that the Lord Jesus said and did on the night in which he was betrayed (*anamnesis*). As spokesman for the congregation he utters the words of thanksgiving (*eucharistia*) and oblation (*anaphora*), in which all the believers may express their gratitude and make the offering of themselves. . . . A worthy minister is one who is so far identified with his people by sympathy and understanding that they can truly participate in the thanksgiving and self-oblation which he makes on their behalf as on his own."[12] As spokesman for the congregation the minister exercises a priestly function but is not in the Old Testament or Roman sense a priest.

SPEAKER FOR GOD

In the third place, the minister speaks not simply for himself or for the congregation, but for God. This viewpoint raises some difficult questions. The current tendency is to soft-pedal this note of authority and to suggest that the minister is preaching only his own thoughts. The Reformed concept, with its emphasis on the authority of the Word of God faithfully proclaimed, is far different. It may be abused. Some ministers have taken one segment of the Word and proclaimed it as though it were the whole of the biblical message. Some ministers unfortunately proclaim their own peculiar isms as the authentic Word of God. On the other hand, some laymen refuse to admit that a minister can know the Word of God any better than they can. One minister who had been treated ruthlessly by a handful of laymen who resented his liberal views on economic, political, and most of all racial questions, wryly asked, "What good is a seminary education if any untrained layman can say his opinion is just as good as the opinion of any theologically trained student?" His question was poorly phrased, but his point was valid. The burden of proof is on the layman who goes against the whole tenor of biblical-theological scholarship on the sort of questions that usually arise, such as, Can a Christian be a segregationist? or, Is Jonah myth or history? or, Do we have an infallible Bible? Every Christian has a right and indeed a duty to form his own opinions. He is not bound to agree with everything a minister says, but he should weigh carefully what his minister preaches. When the preacher is interpreting Scripture to the best of his judgment and in the light of the thought of the church on the matter, the layman is duty-bound to listen thoughtfully before he ignores or scorns the minister's interpretation. Admittedly, Christian scholars can be wrong and a simple layman correct, but this is not an everyday occurrence.

John Calvin thought it arrant nonsense to suggest that untrained laymen need no guidance from carefully trained ministers. "We must allow ourselves to be ruled and taught by men. This is the universal rule, which extends equally to the highest and to the lowest. The church is the common mother of all the godly, which bears, nourishes, and brings up children to God, kings and peasants alike; and this is done by the ministry. Those who neglect or despise this order choose to be wiser than Christ."[13] The average layman today has a much better education than was true in Calvin's time. Many churches have some laymen who are well versed not only in Bible but also in theology. And we need to train still more laymen to be good lay theologians. But even in our day, the minister in most churches is the one person who has had three years of graduate study in theology, and who gives full time to the task of interpreting the Word of God to modern man.

American writers agree that the minister speaks for God. Thomas R. English wrote in 1902: "The work of preaching is the most responsible ever committed to a mortal, and he who has no realizing sense of it thereby gives the strongest evidence of his unfitness for it. Think of that office of 'ambassador,' so gloriously filled by God's eternal Son, and then think of a poor weak mortal taking the place of the only-begotten Son, and acting as the mouthpiece of God in beseeching men to be reconciled to himself!"[14] W. M. Sikes a generation later, in an article on "The Cooperation of the Holy Spirit with the Preacher in Preaching," pointed out that ". . . the preacher of the Gospel has been anointed by Christ with the Holy Spirit for his task. . . . By the help of the Holy Spirit, the preacher, in proclaiming the true message of Christ, utters a divine communication. . . . What both the preacher and his audience need today is a deeper and more profound realization of the fact that he who preaches the Gospel is charged with the responsibility of delivering a divine message. . . . The hearer, too, should receive the preached word as the direct message of God to his own soul."[15] Henry Sloane Coffin writes of the minister who faithfully studies and proclaims the Word: "He is the personal envoy of the all-sufficient God; and his sole aim is to let God draw near in His Word and minister out of His unsearchable riches to needs which He, and He alone, fully understands. His sermon must be an expression of the good news of God, and good news which God Himself speaks in the conscience of each listener." He also wrote: "The preaching of the Word is a corporate action in which preacher, congregation, a long line of their predecessors reaching back through the centuries to the original event and corroborating the interpretation given that event in the Scripture, co-operate. And God is present and active in them all to speak to the man or woman for whom His spirit is seeking."[16]

The minister speaks for God, but only when he is truly unfolding the gospel. The authority with which he preaches is the authority of God when his sermon is a clear proclamation of the Divine message. It is essential for ministers to relate the gospel to the dynamic issues of life, social as well as personal. In moving from principle to application the minister may find himself speaking out of his own cultural background and prejudices rather than out of the Word of God. Historic Christianity, however, has always held to the conviction that ministers who sincerely endeavor to proclaim the meaning of the Word deserve to be listened to with care.

A SERVANT NOT FOR HIRE

The minister is not a hired man. From time immemorial important folk have tried to purchase the voice of the minister. The wealthy Scottish lords had the custom of appointing the ministers, and of controlling them. The Church of Scotland struggled long and hard before it was able to abolish this custom and make its ministers really free.

The emperor, the king, the great nobles, the business tycoon of modern times, have thought they could by means of their power control what the minister said. Sometimes they have succeeded, but fundamentally the ministry has been above purchase. True, even in ordinary congregations ordinary folk in subtle ways have let the minister know that after all they pay his salary. A Swiss layman at Neuchâtel said to William Farel in 1541, "I fire a servant who displeases me, why not a pastor?" And some congregations have stooped so low as to deliberately "starve out" their minister. Fortunately such a vicious attitude is rare. Basically the pulpit is free. No minister is a hired hand, duty-bound to preach what the congregation wants to hear. His loyalty is to his Lord and he must preach the whole gospel with all its implications as he understands those implications. In so doing, he will tread on the toes of some of his people. The minister who never offends any of his people is a man whose sermons are soporific, not stimulating. Most people really do not want their minister to be muzzled. There is stern judgment as well as sheer grace in the gospel, therefore sometimes what the minister says hurts. Prophetic sermons are needed at all times.

Eighty-five years ago R. M. Patterson wrote words that still have pungent meaning. "Perhaps there should be added the duty of our Presbyteries . . . to refuse to permit faithful pastors to be driven from their post by ill treatment. Whatever encourages the people to look at their ministers as hired men, instead of divinely-appointed officers entitled to support, should be frowned upon."[17] He suggested three things that would help: (1) elevate the ministry in the public estimation by maintaining the true view of ordination; (2) elevate the standard of intellectual proficiency in the incumbents in office; and (3) elevate the standards of support. These suggestions continue to be valid!

THE PEOPLE'S ATTITUDE

In the 1960's, as never before, it is imperative that the minister be free. If he speaks for God, he must not be muzzled! As one layman in Louisville put the matter concerning integration, "I don't agree with my pastor, but I know he is right." That attitude is typical of thousands who down deep are proud of their ministers for courageously proclaiming the Word of God, but who are emotionally conditioned against the implications that are so manifestly there.

What, then, should be the attitude of the people to their minister? He is a man, and they know him to be such. They see his weaknesses. They know his wife and children. He is no paragon, and they are aware of that fact. Yet they also know that he is devoted to God. And they know he is not a hired man but God's servant for and through and to the church. The people, therefore, should hear him gladly, obey the gospel which he preaches, and recognize his right to share the rule with the elders. When he speaks for God, the people should obey. But only when he speaks for God!

In the New College Library the writer found a delightful anonymous pamphlet entitled, "Plain Truth; A Seasonable Discourse of the Duties of People to Their Pastors," printed in 1693. The pastor's duty to the people is summarized: to rule or guide, to watch. The people's duty to the pastor is epitomized: to obey, to submit. If that seems too autocratic, listen to these words of wisdom: "It is not the greater Gifts, or Abilities, (whether real, or fancied) of any Minister, that confers a vertue or *Efficacy* to Gospel Ordinances; but it is only the *Blessing* and power of God, conform to his prerogative and promise, that gives the increase and success, Isa. 55:11; I Cor. 3:5, 6, 7. *Therefore* people should neither fondly idolize, nor indiscreetly slight any Godly Minister."[18] The unknown author goes on to say: "The disrespectful Misbehaviours of Unthinking-People towards God's Ministers, their God will resent, as being virtually and constructively, Dishonours and Affronts done to Himself; because he is their Master and Patron, and They are His authorized *Ambassadors* and Commissionat Officers. Luke 10:16 & 2 Chron. 36:15-17."[19]

Positively, people are to consult their pastors when they have "dark and dubious cases" (problems); they should love their pastors; they should obey them when the Word is proclaimed; they should vindicate their pastor's reputation when he is unfairly attacked; they should render cheerfully to their ministers all their just rights and dues ("Ministers are not angels of the Church Triumphant able to live without meat and drink and other corporal comforts");[20] and they should pray much for their minister "who above all men needs to be prayed for."

While the unknown author evinces a lofty view of the ministry, we must keep in mind his "neither fondly idolize." "People," he wrote, "should honour and Reverence their Ministers. Pastors are Spiritual Parents and Ecclesiastical Rulers, and consequently, they are Superiors, to whom both by the Light of Nature and Revelation, Respect and Honour is due. . . ."[21]

The anonymous author shows keen understanding of human nature in his warning not to let your prejudice cause you groundlessly to misconstrue what your pastor says. "Where once Prejudice takes place, the perverse Influence and tincture of this *Black Humour*, Usually inclines to put the Blackest Sence and Gloss upon what the Minister either says or does, and sometimes quite contrare to what he meaned. Ps. 56:5-35."[22]

Principal William Wishart of New College preached to the Scottish General Assembly in 1725 on "Godly Ministers the Strength of the Nation." "We may here be informed of the great folly and madness of these that contemn, hate, revile, and persecute, pious, zealous, and faithful ministers. Such as do so, fight against themselves, and hasten their own ruin, by destroying their chief strength. . . . Then it is the interest of a people who enjoy the great blessing of a pious, zealous, and faithful Gospel Ministry, to esteem them highly, to favour them and to shew kindness to them . . . They are, under God, your best friends and benefactors."[23]

These two quotations are not in the modern mood. The minister is considered to be a father in God, a spiritual parent who is to be obeyed as he proclaims the Word of God. These statements come from men just a hundred years or so out of the Middle Ages, and they still bear the overtones of those years. Beneath the unpopular, undemocratic concept of "superiors" is a truth as pertinent as was the proclamation of the Synod of Missouri, Presbyterian Church in the United States, in 1959, in which they expressed concern that "the pronouncements of our church courts on the social issues confronting us, and the philosophy of the church concerning the ministry of preaching, often become meaningless at the local and Presbytery level." After calling attention to the number of ministers who have been separated from their churches because of their conscientious preaching on social issues, they go on to say: ". . . the heart of the problem lay in the minister daring to speak what he believed was God's truth and will, and interpretation of that truth and will which is in harmony with the church's declared understanding of the teaching of the New Testament, rather than speak in terms of those who would insist that the church and its ministry express the current mood of the congregation."[24]

Christians are not expected to render obedience to ministers as sol-
diers would to the shouted orders of a tough sergeant. The obedience
our ancestors spoke of was really obedience to the pastor insofar as he
proclaimed rightly the Word of God. It is probable that our ancestors
also thought of the pastor as being the "father in God" of the congregation. Three hundred years ago the rank and file of people were less
well educated than in our day, and there were far fewer men of influence to guide the thinking of the people. No radio, no TV, no mighty
newspaper chains told people what to think or do. The pastor then was
a trusted spiritual guide. Insofar as the pastor is a trusted spiritual
guide today, he still should be followed.

Never has the church taught that ungodly ministers are to be
obeyed. Christians have never been expected to follow or obey unworthy, immoral, heretical, or stupid ministers. Nor have they been
expected to follow illiterate or poorly trained men, at least not since
the Reformation. The man in the pulpit is expected to be a godly, well-
trained person.

A MAN OF REAL ABILITY

Principal Wishart proposed in 1725: "Let us take heed whom we
admit to take Part with us in the Holy Ministry. The not adverting to
this as we ought, is like to be the Source or Spring of much Wo and
Misery to this Church. . . . (2 Tim. 2:2) Let us look to it, that the
Church be not pestered with unskilful, or unfaithful, or imprudent
Men, as we will answer upon our Peril to our great Master. . . ."[25]

In 1836, when the Presbyterians were arguing about the quality of
men needed to minister "at the West" (across the Allegheny mountains in Kentucky), an article stated: ". . . the ministers of the west
ought to be men of the first order in intellectual and moral attain-
ments." Genuine piety, acquired knowledge, and mental discipline
were deemed indispensable to the ministers in the West. " 'The priest's
lips should keep knowledge.' Being appointed to teach others, he must
be 'apt to teach,' and 'able to teach;' having himself first learned."[26]
The writer suggested that the church should consecrate the best talent
in the land for this arduous work of winning the West for Christ; that
seminaries should be established and fully endowed (but not too

many!); that candidates should be given a regular and thorough course of studies; and that presbyteries should be more careful in licensing and ordaining candidates.

The General Assembly of 1844 gave the Presbyterian position: "That while the General Assembly feel and proclaim the importance of praying and labouring for an increase of labourers, they do at the same time express their unhesitating belief that men of a high order of talents . . . are now more needed than mere numbers of inferior men . . . and they do most earnestly recommend all the Presbyteries to resist kindly but firmly, the recommendation to the Board of unsuitable candidates, and also to discourage the propensity to hasten into the ministry, without a full course of preparatory study."[27]

In 1916 President J. Ross Stevenson of Princeton Seminary wrote that the present day demands "trained ministers of apostolic character," "men of large positive faith and all aflame with a vital message," with "a theological education equal to the social as well as the individual application of the gospel," men with a missionary outlook.[28]

As early as 1855 a Presbyterian writer was complaining of the buck-passing between presbytery and seminary, whereby unworthy men are ordained. When poor—that is, weak—men are admitted to the ministry, it is difficult to challenge the ablest.[29]

One early American writer summarized it simply: "When we come with *our* offerings, we must bring of our *best*"—our best sons.[30]

I have read hundreds of articles on the ministry. No matter the century, every one says in effect, God wants the best possible men to hear his call and do his work as ministers of Word and Sacrament. The admonition of Paul to Timothy, "Do not be hasty in the laying on of hands" (1 Tim. 5:22), may well be interpreted, ordain no man quickly to the ministry. Be sure, be very sure, before you ordain. Be cautious in accepting candidates; do not expect the seminary to make your decision for you; challenge the best youth to consider the ministry. To seminaries it says, be honest with the candidate and with his presbytery, if there is grave doubt concerning his fitness for the ministry.

In the phrase, "more and better ministers," the key word is "better." The church today does need more ministers, and it needs them badly. But "better" is the primary word, and Reformed thinkers continue to believe that the work of the ordained minister is of such great significance that weak or poorly trained men have no place therein. Hence the recommendation, "resist kindly but firmly unsuitable candidates," is still valid. Every theological seminary in America would say amen to those words. More men, but only more men who are able. God has a place in his ministry for average men, and God can and does empower some average men to do more than average work in the church. Yet mediocrity has little place in the ministry, when the average education of Presbyterian congregations is so high. To fulfill her ministry in the world the church needs able men, today as always.

The minister is one of the *laos*, a member of the people of God. As one of the laity, he, too, is in need of Jesus Christ and his redeeming love. The Word which the minister proclaims he always proclaims to himself as one of the sheep. He is a human being with all the human weaknesses and strengths that other men have. To become a minister does not automatically clothe one with immunity from temptation; in some ways the temptations may increase. Because he is a human being, the minister deserves and needs the sympathy, understanding, love, and comradeship of his people. Inescapably the minister will be judged more severely than other men because he cannot avoid being an example. Called to be an ambassador of the King, the minister must live a life worthy of the gospel he preaches. He is always in need of the prayers of his people.

SELF-IMAGE

How, then, should the minister look upon himself and his office? He should know himself to be a servant, after the example of the Suffering Servant. He should look upon himself as a prophet, whose task is to proclaim fearlessly, but always lovingly, the Word of God to a pagan and perverse generation, and to God's people pilgrimaging in the midst of such a generation. He should know himself to have a priestly function, representing his people before God. He should bear rule in the church, never as an autocrat, and always in conjunction with the elders. He should look upon himself as an ambassador of Christ, proclaiming the Word of reconciliation. He should be a pastor, one who cares for the sheep as did the Good Shepherd.

If he is these things, then without snobbishness, without false pride, in all humility, and graciously, the minister is to be proud not of himself but of his Lord. Not because of what he is in himself but because he is an ambassador of the King, the minister should have a tremendous self-respect. Because he is the bearer of high office in the church of God, he should endeavor above all men to live a life worthy of the gospel, to be a good example. His example is better if it is natural and unconscious rather than deliberately planned and self-conscious. But example he is. Every minister needs to be much in prayer that the Spirit of God will shield him from temptation, or strengthen him in the midst of temptation. He needs in short to be a man of courage, humility, love, unselfish dedication, vision, wisdom, and understanding, a man, indeed, of God.

It is imperative that the minister have the utmost respect for his office. If he does not, the ministry is not his vocation, though it may be his livelihood. The minister does not idolize himself, nor does he allow his people to do so. He knows his own frailty and he prays for pardon and strength and greater spiritual power. He does not think more highly of himself than he ought to think. But he does respect his calling: he is an ambassador of the King! He does not presume upon his office, nor does he lord it over his people. He is their friend, counselor, guide, pastor, father-in-God, but never, never, never a dictator, even in his own daydreams. . . . And the more of a servant he is, the more he will forget himself and his office as he pours his life into his ministerial functions.

VIII

BECOMING A MINISTER

Most denominations have regular ways of approved entry into the ministry. In some of the more extreme sects, however, clearly defined methods of entry into the ministry do not exist. In them, a man may decide on his own initiative that God has called him to be a preacher, and may just start preaching. Many if not most of the "ministers of the gospel" who make the headlines today because of scandalous conduct are actually self-designated ministers, who have no real right to the title. The major denominations have constitutional requirements for entrance into the ministry.

A minister is expected to have a call, a secret call from the Lord to be a minister of the Word. This inner call is known only by the individual. Its reality and validity are testified to by its fruits in the life of the one called. "By their fruits ye shall know them" (Matt. 7:20, KJV). The main-line churches believe that this inner call must be confirmed by an outer call from the church. This outer call usually has two aspects, an examination by proper authorities and a call to a specific service in the church. Variations exist, but the process is clear.

According to most Reformed leaders, an inner call is necessary. Thomas R. English put it, "No one has the right to represent another, or to speak in his name, unless duly authorized to do so. . . . Think of one presuming to offer pardon, without being *commissioned* to do so; or denouncing judgment without express authority from the Lord himself!"[1] God calls a man by choosing him, then telling him he has done so, Dr. English added. This telling is threefold, from his own inner knowledge, from presbytery's approbation following examination, and from the call of a church.

108

THE INNER CALL

Reformed scholars have assumed that a secret call must be a reality in the life of the man who becomes a minister. Calvin writes: "But there is the good witness of our heart that we receive the proffered office not with ambition or avarice, not with any other selfish desire, but with a sincere fear of God and desire to build up the church."[2] The secret call comes in different ways to different men, and there is no standard method by which a youth may determine whether or not he has received a call to the ministry. The call is the inner working of the Spirit, and no man may quickly pass judgment upon how the Spirit works in another man's heart. A presbytery examines a candidate concerning "his motives for seeking the ministry," but only the candidate knows his own heart.

Even he in whose heart the Spirit has planted a call to the ministry may have to struggle to be sure he has such a call. The theological seminaries every year have many candidates who believe they have been called to the ministry but who often wish they had received a clear-cut, absolutely demonstrable call. "If I had just had a vision like Isaiah!" But an Isaiah-type call seldom comes. The Presbyterians of London in 1653 contended that seldom since the days of the apostles has God given an immediate call to a man to enter the ministry. "The mediate ordinary way by which God would have all men to enter into the Ministry is by Election [call of a congregation] and Ordination."[3] God speaks mediately through human influences. Calls come mediately through parents, pastors, teachers, friends, youth conferences, a sense of the great need of the world. The mediate call is not a vision or a voice, but a deep certainty, sometimes slowly reached after an agonized struggle, that one is called of God. "God wants me to be a minister, and to preach his Word." We know it deep inside. And we say, "God has called." "The call consists in the influence of the Holy Ghost enlightening the mind to apprehend the duty, and directing the feelings to desire and seek to be employed by Christ in the holy ministry. . . . Miraculous interpositions, audible voices, dreams, or unaccountable visions, are not to be expected, sought, nor regarded."[4] Thus wrote an anonymous Presbyterian leader in 1831.

Thomas Cary Johnson, a stalwart leader of the Southern Presbyterians for half a century, wrote that while we no longer hear God's call with the bodily sense, "Nevertheless *the Lord continues to call all who should serve him as officers in his church.* . . . the Lord Jesus who is king in Zion calls all his servants whom he would have serve him so, to official functions."[5]

From Puritanism and Pietism there came into Protestantism the idea that the secret call of God to a man to become a minister is all-important. A man will know indubitably that God has called him into the gospel ministry. By clear signs, sometimes of a dramatic nature, he will be firmly assured that God wants him in the ministry. The present generation of seminary students wish they had such a call, but few students today are conditioned to dramatic calls. The truth in the idea of a secret call is that God does not want unbelievers or undedicated persons in the ministry. Gilbert Tennent's famous sermon, "The Danger of an Unconverted Ministry" (1742), though grossly overstated, reminds us of the need for ministers to have a vital relationship to God, to know God's grace in their own hearts, and to believe firmly that he wants them to be ministers.

How do I know I am called to the ministry? By prayerful thought, by deep soul-searching, by listening to the still small voice, by studying my own deepest desires, by looking long and hard at the need of the world and asking how best under God I can help to meet that need, by conferring with wise friends, by feeling such compassion for the hungry multitudes that I want to give them the Bread of Life, by having the proper qualifications—physical, social, and mental—to enable me to do the work, and by studying the indicated leadings of Providence. (Robert L. Dabney rightly warned against reading the signs of providential leading too quickly and too easily!)[6] In time, I just know . . .

THE EXTERNAL CALL

If God has really called a man into the gospel ministry, not only will that man know it deep inside himself, but his knowledge will be confirmed by the church. God calls a man secretly, but he also calls a man externally, through the church. John Holt Rice, founder of Union Theological Seminary in Virginia, wrote in 1826: "The internal call can never exist without the external, but the external may exist without the internal."[7] In effect, a man may delude himself into thinking he has an inner call, but the reality of this call is to be judged by the church as well as by the man. On the other hand, a church may lay its hand on a man, or a church may accept a man, who believes himself to be called when in fact that man has had no true call at all. Foolish men and hypocritical men alike have entered the ministry under the false assumption that God has called them. But men who humbly and sincerely search their own souls concerning the matter seldom go wrong. An external call is also deemed essential, however, because it is possible for self-delusion to occur.

The Reformed tradition lays great stress on the external call. From Calvin on, there has been a conviction *that the church should seek out* able young Christian men and challenge them to consider seriously whether God is calling them to the ministry of Word and Sacrament. The Puritan-Pietist strain in the Reformed churches has been dubious of the validity of this approach, but actually many of the finest leaders of the church have received their call from God to the ministry through the lips of a wise pastor or layman who has seen in them great potential leaders for the church. In our day every major profession diligently recruits qualified men; if the church fails to challenge some of its finest youth, they will assuredly go into a vocation which does challenge them. The church has both the right and the duty wisely and prayerfully to call choice men in the name of God to consider the ministry.[8]

Occasionally a church will lay its hand on a man who is unfit for the ministry. The candidate, the presbytery, and the congregation may all be mistaken about the man's call. When, however, a church refuses to lay hands quickly on a man, when it examines him carefully on his motives for seeking the ministry, when it inquires of his religious experience and of his character, when it counsels him faithfully and prays for him while he is studying for the ministry, when it seeks to weigh his gifts and examine his knowledge, when it tests his theological orthodoxy, and when it does not ordain until he has been properly examined and has been called by a particular church to be its pastor, then just about everything that is humanly possible has been done. And on the whole the results are remarkably good. The call which the man believes he has inwardly received needs the approbation of the sympathetic yet cautious examining body.

The precise nature of the examination which a ministerial candidate receives before he is admitted to the ministry varies with the denomination.[9] Each denomination has a basic pattern for the examination, but the individuals who conduct the examination differ considerably in their approach. In the Presbyterian Church a man who wishes to become a minister first of all must present himself to the session of his own local church—usually after consultation with the pastor. The session examines the young man (or woman), and if it believes him to be sincere, worthy, and qualified, it recommends him to the presbytery to be received as a candidate. Each presbytery has a committee on candidates which examines more thoroughly. This examination includes the person's religious experience and motivation, his physical health, his school record, the forms of Christian service in which he has engaged. Many presbyteries also give the would-be candidate a battery of psychological tests and vocational interest tests. Some even include a psychiatric screening interview, which now is routine for missionary candidates. If the committee approves the candidate, it recommends him to the presbytery for reception as a candidate. Presbytery will expect the candidate to proceed with his studies, which include the securing of a college degree, preferably in the liberal arts, followed by the earning of a theological degree. In theological seminary the student works at the biblical languages, theology, and the other traditional major theological disciplines. His study usually is accompanied by varying degrees of supervised field education, in which he undertakes many of the functions of the minister. Today, more attention is being given to pastoral theology, i.e., to the practical functions of the ministry—preaching, pastoral care, counseling, liturgics, Christian education, church administration. Upon successful completion of his course, a candidate is ready to be examined by his presbytery for ordination. Theological faculties everywhere are struggling with the problem of how to educate their students adequately in too little time.

A man is not normally ordained until he has received a definite call to a particular church or to a specific ministerial function such as minister to a campus or service with a church board. In the Presbyterian Church in the United States, "No Presbytery shall ordain any Candidate to the office of the Gospel Ministry to labor within the bounds of another Presbytery, but shall dismiss him as a Candidate to the Presbytery within whose bounds he expects to labor . . ."[10] The Reformed Church in America has a similar rubric. In the United Presbyterian Church in the U.S.A., however, the candidate "shall ordinarily be examined and ordained by his own presbytery,"[11] though by mutual agreement the examination and ordination may be given by the presbytery to which he has been called. The Presbyterian Church, U.S., recently made it possible for a worthy candidate who wishes to go on to graduate study to be ordained without a call.[12]

The old custom of licensing a man to preach, and requiring him to prove his gifts before ordination, has practically disappeared.

Presbyteries are beginning to take far more seriously their responsibility to examine a person carefully before he is accepted as a candidate for the ministry. Sometimes, however, a mediocre man is recommended by a session which does not wish to offend the faithful parents of the young man. He may be accepted too carelessly by presbytery, and thrust upon the seminary with the pious hope that seminary will fail him. It is also possible for the seminary to graduate that man because he has managed to pass his work, yet wistfully to hope that presbytery will decide not to ordain him. Genuine work needs to be done at this point to the end that fewer mediocre men will slip by presbytery and through seminary and into the ministry. The excuse often given for ordaining weak men is "Somebody has to serve the poor, weak churches." The answer to such a silly argument is that mountain folk and country folk deserve good ministers too, and further, that some of the poor, weak churches would not be so weak if they had good ministers over a period of years.

In the Presbyterian Church, U.S., the candidate for ordination is examined on theology, the sacraments, the English Bible, church government, discipline, and worship. This examination covers his views as well as his knowledge. He is also examined on his Christian experience.[13] In the United Presbyterian Church in the U.S.A., the ordinand is also examined on "the structure, organization, and official programs and promotional policies of the General Assembly . . ."[14] In both denominations his college and seminary diplomas usually are accepted as testifying to his knowledge of philosophy, the biblical languages, and church history.[15] Further, both churches require a thesis on a theological topic, an exegesis of some assigned biblical passage, and a manuscript sermon which normally is to be preached before presbytery. Only in extraordinary cases may presbytery omit any of these parts, and then the exception must be plainly stated in the minutes, with reasons given for the exceptions.

Thus does the church guard itself against intruders into the ministry, whether deliberate or deluded. Thus does the church guard its pulpits against mediocre or unworthy ministers. Sentimentalists often think this process is too demanding, and they insist that any person who believes God has called him into the ministry should be accepted as a candidate and allowed to pass his seminary courses, regardless of the quality of his work. But great as is the need for ministers, it is sheer folly to give in to the sentimentalists. In an age like ours, the ministry is not the place for weaklings, no matter how well intentioned they may be. The gospel ministry calls for the very best leadership the church can produce. The church of today must strengthen her recruiting program to challenge *the most able* youths to consider the gospel ministry.

THE CALL OF THE PARTICULAR CHURCH

The Reformed churches have always frowned upon ordination *sine titulo*. Except for those who are called to specialized ministerial functions—missionaries, teachers, board servants—the church will not ordain a man unless he has a call to a specific pastorate. This particular call is a part of the external call. No man is deemed truly called of God if he does not meet with the approval of fellow Christians, concretely expressed in the form of a call for his ministerial services. The man, the presbytery, and the particular congregation all have to agree that he is called of God to be a minister. If any one of the three fails to approve, the call almost certainly was not of God.

There was a fundamental difference in England between the Independents and the Presbyterians concerning the call, which in the early literature was called "election," to a particular church to be its minister. The Independents (the English Congregationalists and even more strongly the various sects) argued that the essence of becoming a minister is to be elected or called to a particular office, whereas the Presbyterians said that the essence of the minister's call consists in his ordination rather than in his election. Thomas Hooker and other New England brethren (Puritans) were quoted as implying, "Ordination is only . . . an adjunct following and consummating the Ministeriall Call, but not at all entring into the constitution of it: That Ordination is nothing else but the approbation of the Officer, and a setling and confirming him in his Office, and that Election is that which gives him the essentials of his Office."[16] The London Presbyterian ministers showed that the Independents failed to bring a single Scripture passage to prove their point; that the texts they set forth actually prove the Presbyterian point "that the essence of the Ministeriall Call doth consist in Ordination and not in Election. . . ."[17] Election, the Presbyterians insisted, ". . . doth not give him the Office, but the opportunity of exercising his officiall authority over those that choose him. [Acts 6:6.]"[18] Even our New England opponents, they added, in practice do not allow a man elected as pastor to administer the sacraments without ordination.

The nub of their argument was quite important. "If the whole essence of the Ministeriall Call consisteth in Election [to a particular church] then it will follow, that a Minister is only a Minister to that particular charge to which he is called, and that he cannot act as a Minister in any other place."[19] The authors of *Jus Divinum Ministerii Evangelici* took seventeen more pages to pour scorn on this particular idea, which, they insisted, is "unknown in Scripture, unheard of in antiquity, and contrary to sound reason." At that time the Baptists and some other Independents insisted that a minister's ordination only holds good for a particular church, and that when he moves to another church he must be ordained again. Against this narrow concept the Presbyterians rightly insisted, "That Ministers are primarily seated in the Church generall visible, and but secondarily in this or that particular church. . . ." The minister works in the particular church to which he has been elected, "Yet he hath a *virtual* and *habitual* power to preach as a Minister in any place where he shall be lawfully called. . . . They are called Ministers of God, 2 Cor. 6.4, Ministers of Christ. . . . But never Ministers of the people. Indeed they are for the people, but not of the people."[20]

The last sentence was overzealous. Perhaps Samuel Rutherford's statement of the Presbyterian view is more satisfactory. "Ordination maketh a man a Pastor under Christ formally and essentially, the peoples consent and choice do not make him a Minister, but their Minister, the Minister of such a Church; he is indefinitely made a Pastor for the Church."[21] Reordination upon moving to another pastorate is "unscriptural, unhistorical, and unsensible!" This is put rather forcefully: "That every Minister hath a double relation, one to his particular Church [of which he is a minister], another to the Church general visible."[22]

The above paragraphs reveal two basic facts about the Reformed view: The Reformed minister is a minister of the church of Jesus Christ, not merely the minister of X church; and Reformed ministers are not ordained unless they have a call to a definite form of church ministry, this to prevent a ministry being vagrant and ambulatory, lazy and idle, begging and contemptible. . . .[23]

ORDINATION

In the Reformed tradition, ordination is not a mere bit of symbolism. With regard to ordination, as with regard to the sacraments, the Reformed theologians have been about midway between the right-wing Roman Catholics and the left-wing Baptists. Ordination is neither magic nor mummery. It is a deeply meaningful experience in which the promise of God is claimed, and is acted upon by the Holy Spirit. There is no greater moment in the life of a minister than the hour when he is ordained. It is quite likely the deepest spiritual experience of his life. Outwardly he is the same person, but inwardly the Holy Spirit is at work, as he becomes a minister of Word and Sacrament.

Many Reformed thinkers have discussed the nature of ordination. The differences are not as great as one might expect, but there are some subtle distinctions. I shall quote a few of these writers, not in chronological order, but from fairly low church through the mainstream to the high church view, and then, last, Arnold Come, who typifies a number of Americans who believe that new times create new duties and make ancient good uncouth . . .

"The truly Protestant view . . . is that a rite, such as baptism, the

Lord's supper, ordination, does not lie essentially in the *opus opera-tum*, but in the public recognition of an existing fact. . . . Hence they are appropriately called *sealing ordinances*. In ordination these facts are solemnly and publicly recognized: 1. The internal call of the candidate from God to the ministry. 2. The external call from the people to him. 3. The fitness of the candidate, as determined by the vote of the Presbytery after examination and knowledge of him. He is then . . . *set apart* from other men to the office of the ministry."[24] These words, written in 1856, were echoed by Thomas Cary Johnson: ". . . the ordination act was the solemn and formal recognition of the candidate's call, from the people, and from God. . . . together with a formal authentication of him as an officer, and a designation of him before God and his people, as such."[25]

The London Presbyterians in their famous *Jus Divinum* stated that ordination gives the ministerial office only as to the essence of the outward call. ". . . it is the Prerogative Royall of the Lord Jesus to appoint Officers and Offices in his Church. It is Christ onely that institutes the office, and that furnisheth and fitteth men with graces and abilities for the discharge of so great an employment, with willing and ready mindes to give up themselves to so holy services: It is Christ onely that sets the Laws and Rules according to which they must act. All that man doth in Ordination is in a subordinate way as an Instrument under Christ to give the being of an outward Call, and to constitute him an Officer according to the method prescribed by Christ in his Word."[26]

Some three hundred years later the United Church of Canada declared: "(1) Ordination to the ministry is an act of the Church by which a person is solemnly set apart to this office and duty. No man may take this ministry upon himself; there must be an inward call of the Spirit and an outward call and commission by the Church. (2) The power to ordain is vested magisterially in the councils of the Church, with the consent of the people; and ministerially in the presbyters. (3) Ordination is by prayer and the imposition of hands by the presbyters."[27]

Principal George Hill struck a significant note in his classic *Lectures in Divinity*, when he spoke of ordination as ". . . the appointment of Jesus Christ, conveying a character by the instrumentality of the office-bearers of his church. . . . Whenever ordination is considered as the act of Jesus Christ, by his office-bearers constituting a minister of the church universal, the idea of one great society is preserved."[28]

Professor Bannerman's words, written nearly a hundred years ago, are typical of Presbyterianism: ". . . ordination is the solemn act of the Church admitting a man to the office of the ministry, and giving him a right and title to discharge its functions. In all ordinary circumstances it is necessary to a man's entering on the work of the ministry lawfully; and without it he has no authority to exercise the office. It is to be carefully marked that it does not confer the office. Christ confers the office by his own call. . . . But it invests with the office, or admits to it. And in the act of investiture, or admission by the Church with the laying on of hands, and prayer, we have warrant to believe that, in answer to prayer, all the promises connected with the office are fulfilled, and the special blessing or grace suited to the office will be conferred. The act of ordination itself does not, and cannot, confer the blessing as if *ex opere operato* . . . . there are special promises connected with the office of the ministry, and special grace to be warrantably expected by all who are rightly called to the office; and in the act of admission to the office those promises may be claimed in faith, and those graces entreated for; and we have a right to believe that *then* and *there* the promise will be fulfilled, and the grace conferred. This is the only virtue attaching to the ordination, when rightly conferred by the Church and received by the individual. But it is a virtue connected with it, and not to be enjoyed without it. . . . Ordination is less than a charm, but it is more than a form."[29]

Bishop Lesslie Newbigin of the Church of South India, a leader in the ecumenical movement and ordained in the Church of Scotland, has given an excellent statement. Pastors "are, indeed, representatives of the local church. But they are at the same time representatives of Christ to the Church. They have a commission from Him which requires that while they serve the flock they have also the authority to rule and teach. That belongs to the character of the ministry as the Church has always understood it. It is given to them in ordination. Ordination is an act of the Church done in faith towards her living Head, in the faith that He hears her prayer and 'bestows upon and assures to those whom He has called and the Church has accepted for any particular form of the ministry, a commission for it and the grace appropriate to it.' "[30]

G. W. Sprott, leader of the high church wing of the Church of Scotland at the turn of the century, wrote: "The Christian Church in all ages has held that several ministers should take part in ordination, and that it is irregular, though not necessarily invalid, when done by a single person . . . . the powers of the office are not conferred by the ordainers, any more than is the grace of Sacraments imparted by those who administer them. The powers of the Christian Ministry were conferred by the Head of the Church once for all, and though coming through appointed channels, they descend from Him upon the person ordained, who is admitted to a participation of them in virtue of the office with which he is regularly invested."[31]

We move into another world when we read Professor Come's able book, *Agents of Reconciliation.* Most of his points are sound, but his main point is questionable. "It is high time," he writes, "that every Christian communion or denomination completely reformed its entire theory and practice of ordination. If the church is to retain this formal mode of recognition and control, then it must at least do the following: (1) practice ordination in a way that does not exalt one class of Christians to a qualitatively different rank, thus absolutizing the clergy-laity distinction; (2) recognize the variety of ministries in the church and that ordination will always apply to more than *one*; (3) leave it an open and relative question as to the extent of ordination among the various ministries . . ." Dr. Come's passionate concern for the unity of the church is admirable. He goes too far, however, for what he urges would complete the denigration of the concept "minister." "If every member is a minister in the church, then we must cease referring to one group of members as ministers, or as comprising *the* ministry of the church. Indeed, they are ministers but just as all other members also are ministers. They are not qualitatively or personally different or unique; they are only *functionally* unique. But every other member is also functionally unique in that he shares in one or more forms of ministry that are not shared in by all other members. Not everyone shares equally in every ministry, no one shares in every ministry, everyone shares more intensively in one or several ministries than in others."[32]

The whole country knows the value of genuine leadership for the
nation. And most laymen know the worth of having a minister who is
the minister set by Christ in the church for the equipment of the saints
for the work of ministering. The Reformed view of ordination is not
designed to create an antithesis between laity and clergy. The Presbyterian concept has been that church members accept and acknowledge
and set apart this particular man, the gift of Christ to the church, as
a pastor and teacher. No wise Christian leader, since the Reformation
at least, has ever really thought that ministers are qualitatively different from laymen. Ordination does say to the world: This man is
chosen of God and approved of the church and set apart to be a minister of Word and Sacrament, to devote his life full-time to the service
of the church. In a sense all Christians live full-time lives of Christian
service. This is the service of the laity. But the need of the specific
work of one who is pastor and teacher is quite clear. At the moment of
writing this, I am serving as moderator of a church whose former
pastor stressed during his pastorate the ministry of the laity. This
church has some remarkable Christian leaders; several elders actually
live up to the highest dreams of what an elder should be. They really
do pastoral and evangelistic work as well as living their professional
lives in a manner worthy of the gospel. These men do not believe that
ordination has a bad effect upon the relationship between pastor and
people. The laymen are bearing the burden of the work of the church.
But in grave emergencies they call upon their minister, and they do
not feel themselves to be second-grade Christians when they do so.

A few stuffed-shirt-type ministers might fall deservedly under
Come's castigations, but in general pastors do not think of themselves
as "better" than their parishioners. The writer has met few people
who feel about the laity-clergy relationships as Dr. Come thinks they
do.[33] Ordination is still essential to the well-being of the church. Instead of emptying the word minister of all meaning, we had better
restore its richness of meaning. All Christians partake of the ministry
of the church, but God has set apart some in the church for the ordained ministry. The time is ripe for many changes in the life of the
church, but the derogation of the ordained minister is not one of them.

In the Bible, in the whole history of the church, and in the writings
of all the Reformed thinkers, ordination is conceived to be less than

magic but far more than mere form. Both to the church and to the
candidate it is such a deeply meaningful experience that it ought to be
continued. The church must retain its right to determine the quality
and the basic theology of its ministers, and this is best done through
something very close akin to the Presbyterian system of examination
and ordination, following call.

Only a man with ice in his veins could fail to be deeply moved by
ordination. In the Form and Order for the Ordination to the Holy
Ministry, the moderator makes a tremendous statement of the faith of
the Presbyterian Church as a part of the church universal, thus asserting that the man to be ordained becomes a minister of the Holy Catholic Church. The candidate answers the constitutional questions, then
comes the ordination prayer, the heart of which is, "Send down Thy
Holy Spirit upon this Thy servant, whom we, in Thy name and in
obedience to Thy holy will, do now by the laying on of our hands
[here hands are laid upon the head of the ordinand] ordain and appoint to the office of the holy ministry in Thy Church, committing
unto him authority to preach the Word, administer the Sacraments,
and to bear rule in the Church." Following the prayer, the moderator
proclaims the ordinand to be duly ordained, and then the presbyters
give him the right hand of fellowship, "to take part of this Ministry
with us." Then follows a solemn charge to the new minister.[34]

This is no mere form! God is at work in ordination! Lesslie Newbigin's words concerning the ordination prayer in the Church of
South India make a fitting climax to this discussion: "The prayer is
the prayer of the whole Church and the hands are the hands of the
whole Church which is His Body—not only of those now present, not
even of those now living, but of all who have gone before everywhere
and always. It is the hands that bear the unmistakable authority and
commission of the whole Church that must be laid on the head of the
ordinand, in token that the prayer that is offered is in truth the prayer
of the whole Church—is indeed, 'through Jesus Christ our Lord,' a
part of the one undiscordant offering of perpetual prayer which is
made by Christ and by the Church in Him. The double nature of the
Church is here made vividly clear. The Church appoints, ordains,
commissions. It does so 'in the name of Christ.' But that is not a mere
formula, nor does the Church act as the attorney of an absent Prin-

cipal. Her act is a prayer to Him to act (for He alone can give what is to be given), and her prayer is an act which is thenceforth recognized as an act of the Body of Christ in all its consequences (for His will is to be done upon earth). The man so ordained is not merely the representative organ of the Church. He is the representative of Christ to the Church, possessed of the authority to speak and act for Him to His Church."[35]

THE LAYING ON OF HANDS

All that is necessary to declare a man a minister is for the presiding officer of the examining body to state formally that the man is now admitted to the ministry. Both Calvin and Knox recognized that due to the inherited superstition connected with the rite of laying on of hands, it could be dispensed with, though they thought it to be biblical and sound. The church has nearly always accompanied the act of admission to the ministry with prayer and the imposition of hands. A man can be made a minister without either, but both are biblical, traditional, and sensible. In earlier years fasting was also an important part of the backdrop of ordination. Fasting has, however, dropped out of the religious life of Protestants. The appropriateness of prayer is manifest. Our Lord himself prayed before calling the twelve apostles. We are not certain that Jesus laid hands upon the apostles in ordination. The apostles practiced the laying on of hands. Almost certainly, prayer was offered before or during all significant acts of the church, including the choice of and ordination of church officers.

The laying on of hands has an Old Testament background. It was "a ritual gesture by which a man transmits his own characteristics, his personality, to an animal (cf. Lev. 1:3-4; Exod. 29:10, etc.) or to certain men (the Levites, Num. 8:10), so as to bring about a substitution of persons, i.e., to be validly represented in the cultus by such an animal sacrificed, or by the Levites in the service of the Temple."[36] The concept of consecration, or setting apart for God, is also found in the Old Testament, as for instance, when Moses laid hands upon Joshua (Num. 27:18 and Deut. 34:9). In Jewish ritual at the time of Christ, apparently there was imposition of hands upon church officers. In the New Testament, laying on of hands is used in three circum-

stances: (1) in the healing of the sick (Mark 6:5; Luke 13:13, etc.);
(2) in baptism (Heb. 6:2; Acts 19:1-7, etc.); and (3) in the setting
apart or consecration of men to the ministry. It is this latter usage
which is primarily relevant to our discussion. The most significant passages are given herewith.

In Acts 6:1-6 is related the appointment of seven men of good
repute to assist the apostles—whether they were the prototype of our
modern deacons or elders for the Greek-speaking Christians matters
little. "These they set before the apostles, and they prayed and laid
their hands upon them" (Acts 6:6; see also Acts 13:2-3).

The words of Paul to Timothy are particularly important, no matter what view is taken of the authorship or date of the Pastoral Epistles. "Do not neglect the gift you have, which was given you by prophetic utterance when the elders [better, the presbytery?] laid their
hands upon you" (1 Tim. 4:14). This clearly implies that Timothy
was ordained by a group of presbyters, and that upon his ordination
he received a gift which could only have come from God, not directly
from the presbyters. That gift was the power of the Holy Spirit in his
life. "Do not be hasty in the laying on of hands" (1 Tim. 5:22) has
traditionally been interpreted as meaning, "Ordain no man hastily."
"Hence I remind you," wrote Paul to Timothy, "to rekindle the gift of
God that is within you through the laying on of my hands; for God
did not give us a spirit of timidity but a spirit of power and love and
self-control" (2 Tim. 1:6-7). Again, hands, ordination, gift—the spiritual gift coming from the empowerment of the Holy Spirit. This
particular verse speaks of the laying on of hands of the presbytery
(1 Tim. 4:14) as indicating that Paul along with the other presbyters
laid hands on Timothy. The issue is clear. Is ordination by one man, a
bishop, or is it by a presbytery, composed of presbyter-bishops? Early
church history seems to agree with the Reformers at this point, but our
knowledge is not complete. The question is intricate.

While we have no biblical command that makes it necessary to lay
hands upon ordinands, we do have a clear-cut biblical example. It is of
the *bene esse* of the church that ordination be with prayer and the
laying on of hands. And the prayer is even more important than the
imposition of hands.

WHOSE HANDS?

The Westminster Standards, *circa* 1645, state that the laying on of hands is to be by "the preaching presbyters to whom it doth appertain." The London Presbyterians were equally emphatic on this point. The Provincial Assembly ruled: "That the power of ordering of the whole work of Ordination belongs to the whole Presbytery, that is, to the Teaching and Ruling Elders. But Imposition of Hands is to be alwayes by Preaching Presbyters, and the rather, because it is accompanied with Prayer and Exhortation, both before, in, and after, which is the proper work of the Teaching Elder."[37]

Present-day opinion on the matter is divided. The writer recently questioned a number of leading Scottish ministers. One, the retiring moderator of the General Assembly that year, and a distinguished church historian, was of the opinion that only preaching elders should impose hands on the ordinand; another, an equally distinguished theologian, took the opposite position, that it would be good for the entire presbytery to participate in the laying on of hands. Neither considered this a supremely important matter. From the beginning, ruling elders in the Presbyterian Church, U.S., have participated in the laying on of hands. In the United Presbyterian Church in the U.S.A., ruling elders do not participate. The lines were drawn on this matter well over a hundred years ago. At the General Assembly of 1843 the matter came to a head. That Assembly overwhelmingly voted (yea 138, nay 9), "That it is the judgment of this General Assembly, that neither the Constitution, nor the practice of our Church, authorizes Ruling Elders to impose hands in the ordination of ministers."[38] Of the nine nays, five were from Kentucky, two of these being ruling elders, one from Tennessee, and two from the synod of Georgia-South Carolina, one an elder. The fifth elder was from Illinois. The fiery Robert J. Breckinridge carried on a virile magazine warfare against the majority decision. In 1844 the question was up again; and again the vote was overwhelmingly to maintain the old custom: for, 154 (60 ruling elders, 94 ministers) ; against, 25 (13 ruling elders, 12 ministers). The 1844 Assembly softened the bluntness of the 1843 decision by saying: "*Resolved*, That in the opinion of this Assembly, the last Assembly in determining that Ruling Elders are not authorized by the form of government to impose hands . . . did not depreciate the office of Ruling Elder, nor did they in any respect contravene the letter or the spirit of the constitution . . . but in conformity with both the principles and practice of our own and other Presbyterian Churches, they did decide that as the rite of ordination is simply a declaratory ministerial act, the laying on of hands as a part thereof belongs properly to ordained Ministers, while to Ruling Elders is left unimpaired and unquestioned the full and rightful power of ordering the work of ordination, and of judging in the discipline of ministers in common with those Presbyters who labour in word and doctrine as in all other cases."[39]

When the Southern ("U.S.") Presbyterian Church came into existence, the brilliant James H. Thornwell, who already had taken up the cudgels along with Breckinridge, was instrumental in making it clear that ruling elders should join in the imposition of hands.

I have participated in a fair number of ordination services in both major Presbyterian denominations in America. In my judgment, whether ruling elders do or do not participate is not a matter of tremendous importance. I agree with the logic of Hodge and the custom of the church, that only those who hold a particular office can induct another into that office. Yet there is a great deal to say for having the representatives of the people participate in ordination. Logically and historically, Hodge was right and Breckinridge and Thornwell were wrong. But psychologically, in a democratic world where anti-clericalism already exists in too many places, the Presbyterians can do much to lessen this anti-clericalism by allowing the ruling elders to impose hands as well as judicially to determine that a man is worthy of being ordained. Theologically, something can be said for the concept that ordination as an act of the whole church calls for the participation of ruling elders. Ministers are more truly laymen than ruling elders are ministers (except in the current ambiguous use of the term), but ruling elders are truly representatives of the people, whereas ministers are not basically representatives of the people but of God. (Of course ministers are human beings too, but God has called them and the church has ordained them to an office-function that is in a way unique, as God's ambassadors.) It is good, then, for the entire body to participate in ordination, and this can best be done symbolically by the representatives of the people, the ruling elders, participating in the imposition of hands. Beyond question, the most important thing is not who impose hands, but whether the Holy Spirit is present. I have felt his presence both in services north of the Ohio River and in services south of that beautiful, dividing stream.

IX

THE REFORMED MINISTER:
PLACE AND POWERS

PARITY

Parity is a distinctive feature of the Reformed view of the ministry. All ministers are equal, all presbyters are on the same plane, so far as powers are concerned. Every presbyter is a local bishop, and every bishop has the power to ordain, to admit to the church, and to proclaim the Word through sermon and sacrament. Most Presbyterians do not believe in having bishops who hold ecclesiastical rank above their fellow presbyters. From time immemorial presbyters were equal, and at the beginning all presbyters participated in ordinations. Presbyterians do not deny the right of a bishop to ordain, for he is himself a presbyter, and as a presbyter he has this right inalienably. Presbyterians deny the necessity of having prelatical bishops (men accorded superior rank and dignity). They do not deny the possible superior efficiency of a system of bishop-superintendents, as in the Presbyterian Church of Hungary or as in the Scottish Church in the days of John Knox. But when a Presbyterian denomination chooses a man to be a bishop over a region (all parish ministers are bishops of their own parish) he continues to be simply a presbyter, who is chosen by his brethren for purposes of leadership and efficiency, not because the unity and orthodoxy and continuity of the church depend on a lineal series of bishops. Presbyterian parity contrasts sharply with Episcopal order. All Presbyterian ministers are equal, but among the Episcopalians there are three ranks of clergy: deacons, presbyters, and bishops. Union between these two great denominations will be difficult to accomplish unless this difference in status of ministers is resolved. Reformed theologians still believe that each pastor is as fully a minister of Jesus Christ as is any other. John Calvin made clear his convictions about prelacy and the equality of ministers, when he commented on 1 Peter 5:1, "So I exhort the elders among you, as a fellow elder . . ." Said Calvin: "Since Peter calls himself in like manner a *presbyter*, it appears that it was a common name . . . Moreover, by this title he secured for himself more authority, as though he had said that he had a right to admonish pastors, because he was one of themselves, for there ought to be mutual liberty between colleagues. But if he had the right of primacy he would have claimed it . . . But though he was an Apostle, he yet knew that authority was by no means delegated to him over his colleagues, but that on the contrary he was joined with the rest in the participation of the same office."[1] The Second Helvetic Confession, 1566, has the following statement: "There has, moreover, been given to all ministers in the Church a like and equal power or function. Certainly, from the beginning, bishops or elders have governed the Church in a service shared together; nobody has set himself before another, or has usurped for himself an ampler power and dominion among his fellow bishops. . . ."[2] Thomas Cartwright and John Udall, English Presbyterians, held similar views. J. L. Ainslie quotes Udall to this effect: "But Christe hath directly forbidden, that one minister should have dominion over another (Matt. xx.25; Luke xxii.25). Therefore one minister may not have superiority or dominion over another . . . Equall power and function is given to all ministers of the Church . . ."[3] The struggles of the Scottish Church with the kings were highlighted more than once by the question of equality. In 1584 the king sought to make all ministers promise to be submissive to him, and to his appointed bishops. Nine ministers made vigorous protest, "As tuiching the intituled Archbishop of St. Andrewes, called in the letter our ordinar, we answere, that we can not with good conscience obey him in suche as he pretendeth, for these causes following: First, nather the titles of Archbishop, nor ordinar, can we find agreeable to the Word of God . . . . it is against the Scriptures to a man to claime superioritie above his brother, who are yocke fellowes with him in the ministrie, and office of teaching."[4] In kindred vein *The Second Buik of Discipline* of the Church of Scotland emphatically rejected "all the ambitious Titles inventit in the Kingdome of Antichrist."[5]

In the family of Reformed Churches (1) all ministers are deemed to be of equal rank, and (2) for the sake of order, one man is designated or elected to preside over meetings.

The doctrine of the equality of ministers was never intended to suggest that all ministers are equal in talent or piety or vision or scholarship or courage or wisdom. This doctrine of equality is a matter of official status, ability to have free vote and voice, and equal powers. Wherever human beings gather, some appear to have more natural leadership ability than others. Geneva had its John Calvin, Zurich its Zwingli and its Bullinger, Basel its Oecolampadius, Scotland its John Knox and its Andrew Melville. All ministers are equal in the same sense that all men are equal, a sense which denies neither individuality nor native ability.

Ainslie shows convincingly that the Scottish superintendents differed greatly from prelatic bishops, though they had the power of ordaining, which was not granted to the local bishops or pastors.[6] The Scottish superintendents did not control the church but were controlled by the church, much as a presbytery executive secretary in the American church is controlled by his presbytery council. Both Knox and Melville, incidentally, were invited to assume bishoprics but declined, Knox in 1552, Melville in 1607.

The moderator of a church court such as the presbytery or the General Assembly is simply a presiding officer. Inevitably a touch of "honor" attaches to the office. At first, because of their dislike of prelacy, the Scottish Presbyterians were very careful to state that a man was chosen as moderator simply for the purpose of good order, not because he was superior in rank to the other ministers. But he who is moderator of a General Assembly cannot avoid being *primus inter pares*. His brethren have chosen him to assume office, and in that office to a degree he symbolizes "the church." He does not have the powers of a prelate, but men everywhere honor him because he has been elected moderator. In the Scottish Church today, when the moderator enters the Assembly Hall all stand, and not until he has formally bowed first to the Queen's Lord High Commissioner, and then to each section of the Assembly, do the members take their seats. In the Presbyterian Church, U.S., when the moderator appears on the platform or rises to speak at a special meeting, all present rise in silent tribute to him as a person, to his office, to his church, and to the Lord whom he represents. No Presbyterian looks upon his moderator as a prelate in whom the unity, purity, and orthodoxy of the church are preserved, but the moderator is looked upon as a man to be honored by virtue of his office, which was given to him because of his service to the church. He is still, however, simply a presbyter with one vote. If an ex-moderator can influence other votes in meeting, it is because he is a five-talent or a ten-talent man, and not because he is a prelate.

MINISTERIAL POWERS

The respective Forms of Government of the two large American Presbyterian Churches define the powers of the minister from two angles, first from his titles, second from his duties.[7] The Presbyterian minister has three main powers or rights. He has committed to him at ordination "authority to preach the Word, administer the Sacraments, and to bear rule in Thy Church."[8]

1. In the Reformed church family, only ordained ministers may administer the sacraments. As early as the Genevan Ordinances, 1541, the two sacraments were to be administered only by the ministers. Concerning the superstitious custom of midwives baptizing infants, Calvin said, "I hold that whosoever baptizes without a lawful call, rashly intrudes into another's office. . . . For that office of the gospel which he assigns to ministers, women seize to themselves."[9]

The Scots Confession of 1560 affirmed: "That Sacramentis be richtlie ministrat, we judge twa things requisite: the ane, that they be ministrat be lauchful Ministers, whom we affirme to be only they that ar appoynted to the preaching of the word. . . ."[10] The First and Second Books of Discipline, the Westminster Standards, and all other Reformed documents are in agreement. Calvin's Catechism put the matter:

"366. MINISTER: *To whom belongeth the ministration of Baptisme, and of the Lordes Supper?*

CHILD: Unto them who have the charge to preach openly in the Church: for the preaching of Gods worde, and the ministration of the Sacramentes be things jointly belonging to one kinde of office."[11]

Ainslie sagely points out, "Thus the prerogative of the minister to be the sole dispenser of the sacraments rests upon the fact that he is the authorised preacher."[12]

2. "The power of the keys" is judged by all the Reformed churches to be an inalienable part of the function of the minister. The precise meaning of the keys has been a controversial topic for centuries. The Westminster Confession of Faith speaks for Presbyterians: "The Lord Jesus, as king and head of his church, hath therein appointed a government in the hands of church officers . . . To these officers the keys of the kingdom of heaven are committed, by virtue whereof they have power respectively to retain and remit sins, to shut that kingdom against the impenitent, both by the word and censures; and to open it unto penitent sinners, by the ministry of the gospel, and by absolution from censures, as occasion shall require" (XXXII. I, II).

The gospel publicly preached opens or shuts the doors of the Kingdom. He who proclaims the word of salvation offers a man the opportunity to shut the door in unbelief or to open it in faith. In preaching the word of reconciliation, the minister is using the keys. He says in effect to the people, If you believe, I give you the key to salvation. Ultimately it is the Word which says, Believe and be saved.

The power of the keys is often equated with church discipline. The church officers exercise the power of the keys through discipline, which is never by the minister alone but is always shared with the session. When the session decides to excommunicate a member, which happened more frequently in the past than today, the moderator makes public the judgment of the session. If a repentant sinner satisfies the session of his change of heart and is received back into the Christian fellowship, again it falls to the minister to announce the fact publicly. Church discipline in strict or rigid fashion has largely disappeared from the life of the major churches. There are those who insist that the work of pastoral care, and counseling in particular, may be the modern counterpart of old-fashioned church discipline. The point has some validity. Many things which our ancestors deemed to be due to human sinfulness we know to be due to human frailty at the psychological level. Yet those who know human nature best seem to believe that some if not most psychological difficulties in the beginning had spiritual roots. In any case, church discipline is never vindictive punishment but is thought of as being for the reformation of the offender. "They [the Church] must beware, and take good heed, that they seem not more ready to expel from the Congregation, than to receive again those in whom they perceive worthy fruits of repentance to appear: neither yet to forbid him the hearing of Sermons, who is excluded from the Sacraments and other duties of the Church, that he may have liberty and occasion to repent."[13]

Individual Reformed ministers do not have the right to excommunicate. Calvin is typical. "Moreover I have never thought it useful to entrust the right of excommunicating to single pastors. For the thing is odious, of doubtful example, apt to merge into tyranny, and the Apostles have transmitted to us a contrary practice."[14]

Ministers themselves are under discipline. Just as Luther found it necessary to send out visitors to check on the quality of work and the character of his new ministers, so Calvin and Knox found it desirable to have regular gatherings wherein the minister was counseled and even disciplined by his colleagues. In Scotland at the very beginning, the session of the churches of a community could discipline a minister. Later, discipline of ministers came to be the prerogative of presbytery and was taken away from the local session. If a minister is deemed immoral or heretical, or even foolish, by his session or by some members of his congregation, the matter may be taken up by his peers in presbytery. (Actually the early Scottish city session was more like a presbytery than like a local church session.) Ministers, too, need discipline, and presbytery disciplines them. Some ministers unfortunately are inclined to be harsh in their judgments of their fellow ministers, and are all too quick to condemn them upon rumor, spread sometimes by irresponsible persons. Presbytery is composed of ruling elders—laymen—as well as ministers. This is a wise procedure, for often the minister will receive deeply sympathetic understanding from ruling elders who "can discern the things that differ."

Roman Catholic priests have a third way in which they exercise the power of the keys. That is in the confessional, after which they have the power to pronounce absolution. In general, Protestants disavow the private confessional, though a number of Protestant churches place in their order of corporate worship public confession with assurance of pardon. John Calvin in particular made use of Scriptural declarations of pardon and in his Strasbourg order, 1539, actually pronounced absolution. The voluntary confessional in the form of pastoral counseling has proved to be of great value to many persons. The minister can and should give assurance of pardon where there is guilt confessed and repented of in trust toward Jesus Christ.

3. Ministers have the power to bless the people. The London Provincial Assembly said, "It belongs to them . . . to pray for and blesse the people in the Name of God."[15] *The Second Buik of Discipline* phrased it, "It apperteinis be the same Reason to the Pastors to pray for the People, and namely for the Flock committed to his Charge, and to blesse them in the Name of the Lord, who will not suffer the Blessings of his faithfull Servants to be frustrat."[16]

The American Presbyterian custom has been that only the minister should pronounce the Apostolic or the Aaronic benediction. He does not say, "May the grace of the Lord Jesus Christ and the love of God and the fellowship of the Holy Spirit . . . be with us" but rather he says, "The grace . . . be with you." The benediction is not a prayer, it is a blessing. The blessing contains no magical power, but it is the proclamation, by God's chosen and set-apart minister, of God's grace for his people. The current disregard of this ancient custom may be due to ignorance.

4. The ordained minister alone has the authority to perform the marriage ceremony. There was a time when some among the Puritans denied this privilege to their ministers, but essentially it has been the accepted right of ministers to hear the vows of their people in marriage. The minister, like the magistrate, is a servant of the body politic when he performs a wedding. A few Protestants, legalistic in their anti-legalism, have objected to this, but not many. In the truest sense, the couple by their vows marry themselves, with the sanction of the state, which for public order and decency licenses them to marry, and with the blessing of the church through its minister. The ordained minister prays for the blessing of God upon the marriage. Today the minister also gives premarital counseling, and if necessary postmarital counseling as well.

5. The chief power the minister possesses is to be a minister of the Word. Chapter X of the Book of Church Order of the Presbyterian Church in the United States is entitled "The Minister of the Word."

During the Reformation, and for long years afterward, his chief function was indeed to preach the Word. It has always been recognized
that a minister preaches not only with his lips but also with his life,
not only from the pulpit but in everything he does. And always it has
been understood that sacraments are the visible Word. Often the minister is called the minister of Word and Sacrament. His two distinctive functions are preaching and administration of the sacraments.
With the other elders he governs the church. It is true that today the
average minister may consider his pastoral work to be his most important function, and pastoral counseling has become for some ministers
their chief joy. Nevertheless, pastoral work is not uniquely the work
of the minister, but preaching is. And if he allows counseling to take
too large a share of his time and interest, he may well have chosen the
wrong profession—the minister just ought not to try to be a psychiatrist!

In an era when, and a country where, some two million Sunday
school teachers each Sunday "teach the Word," it may be a bit hard
to realize that the Reformed tradition has strongly insisted that only
ordained ministers preach the gospel. As James D. Smart has shown, a
great deal of this teaching by volunteer, untrained laymen has been
pathetic, often nothing but stifling moralisms. "The Bible stories are
consistently used, and often twisted to make them useful, to point a
moral . . . Moralism bores us because it confronts us with an impossi-
bility."[17] And, one must add, the concern for biblical facts, divorced
from searching for meaning, has driven many an active young thinker
away from the church, at least for a while. Wesner Fallaw's proposed
solution that we recruit many more ministers, about one for every
eighty families, and expect these ministers to teach the adults and
youth of the church at fairly serious levels, leaving Sunday school for
the little ones, is unrealistic and too drastic.[18] As teacher, the pastor's
basic task is to teach the church officers and adults of the church the
meaning of the Christian faith in depth. Fallaw is correct in his thesis
that most ministers spend entirely too much of their time doing organizational and administrative work which capable laymen could do
at least as well and probably much better, and that these ministers
have a divine obligation to *teach* their people the meaning of the
Christian faith. Recent educational theory that "the entire church

teaches" is true within limits, and certainly ministers can learn many things both spiritual and secular from their laymen. Nevertheless, it is a rare congregation in which any layman is as well equipped as is the minister to unfold the unsearchable riches of the gospel. The minister has no greater power, no higher responsibility, no more vital function, than to proclaim, by teaching and preaching, the Word. It is the teaching of the Word which gives the minister his authority, which ceases when he betrays the Word or when he relies primarily upon personality and character and not upon the Word.

In the Reformed tradition, in addition to ordained ministers, only probationers or candidates for the ministry may preach. While the probationer is a layman, he is trying out his gifts that the church may judge whether or not he has the qualities that will fit him for the ministry. Well into the twentieth century the tradition still held that only ordained ministers preach the gospel. Perhaps the church has been right to encourage elders to "preach" in vacant churches. The choice was either this or the establishment of a system of lay preachers. The error is not in asking elders to preach but in asking them to preach without adequate training. Far more serious is the way college students, long before they have received adequate education in the Bible and theology, go out and "preach" regularly. An occasional devotional talk is good, but regular preaching on the part of untrained students is unwise. A few students by virtue of rare gifts and an apt tongue may do much good this way, albeit they may develop bad habits of preparation and proclamation. Preaching the gospel is the most important task of the church and it is not lightly to be entrusted to untrained men. The pulpit still needs to be shielded from ignorance and immaturity, no matter how good the intentions.

THE SOURCE OF CHURCH POWER

All Christians are agreed that Jesus Christ is the Head of the church and therefore the source of its power. When this fundamental principle is translated into practice, differences begin to emerge. Romanists believe that Christ has appointed a vicar, the Pope, through whom his power comes into the church. Anglicans tend to see this power as being inherent in the bishops who by lineal descent are from the Apostles. Congregationalists of all varieties see that power inherent in the congregation. Presbyterians have been of two minds on the matter.

There is a high church Presbyterianism which locates the powers of the church in the officers of the church. Rutherford, strong friend of the elders, concluded "That the keys of discipline were committed not to the Church, but to the officers of the Church." And "Christ gave the keys not to the Church mystical, but to the Church ministerial, including authority to preach and baptize."[19] Robert Baillie's unprinted manuscript lectures in the University of Glasgow Library give "a brief refutation of Independency, wherein it is showed that the power of Church government is in the church officers, and not in the body of the Church."[20] Two centuries later Principal George Hill wrote: "Persons vested with church government derive their powers, not from the people, but from Jesus Christ by his ministers."[21]

American Presbyterians have been more cautious concerning church powers. Those in the South have been unconsciously influenced by the burgeoning Baptists with their strong emphasis on the power of the congregation. Charles Hodge was something of a mediator between the high church Scots and the low church Americans. During "the elder controversy" in the 1840's, Hodge stalwartly opposed Breckinridge and Thornwell, asserting that the power to ordain lies in the ordained ministry itself. Hodge, however, also stated: "Protestants unite in teaching that all church power vests radically not in the clergy as a class, but in the Church as a whole. . . . The power of the keys, therefore, vests ultimately or primarily in the people; of which power they can never rightfully divest themselves."[22] He fully realized the paradox involved. "It is thus that the apostle reconciles the doctrine that ministers derive their authority and power from Christ, and not from the people, with the doctrine that Church powers vest ultimately in the Church as a whole. He refers to the analogy between the human body and the Church as the body of Christ [each member receiving gifts according to the will of Christ]. . . . So that ministers are no more appointed by the Church, than the eye by the hands and feet." According to the New Testament, ". . . the ministers of the Church are the servants of Christ, selected and appointed by him through the Holy Ghost." "They speak in Christ's name, and by his authority. They are sent by Christ to the Church, to reprove, rebuke, and exhort with all long-suffering and doctrine. They are indeed the servants of the Church, as labouring in her service, and as subject to her authority—servants as opposed to lords—but not in the sense of deriving their commission and powers from the Church."[23]

The Presbyterian Church in the United States, in good Presbyterian tradition, emphatically says that Jesus Christ is the King and Head of the Church. "It belongs to his Majesty from his throne of glory, to rule and teach the Church, through his Spirit and Word, by the ministry of men, thus mediately exercising his own authority, and enforcing his own laws, unto the edification and establishment of his kingdom."[24]

Christ rules his church "by the ministry of men." The main Presbyterian tradition has interpreted this to mean by the church officers. The low church Presbyterians, led by Thornwell, have tended to stress that the rule is by the corporate priesthood of believers—the whole body. Extreme high churchism leads to clericalism, extreme low churchism becomes congregationalism, neither of which is true to Reformed theory. The present statement in the Book of Church Order is a compromise between the extremes of interpretation. "The power which Christ has given his Church is wholly moral and spiritual." It "rests not in individuals but in the Church as a whole." This principle avoids the danger of clericalism. Section 1-3 goes on to state that "the exercise of Church power has divine sanction only when in conformity with the Word." The last section of chapter 1 makes it clear that while power ultimately vests in the entire church, operationally it is exercised by the church officers—particularly the minister.

"Church power is exercised both by church members and by Church officers. It is exercised by the members of a church in choosing those whom Christ calls to office in his Church. It is exercised by Church officers individually, as in preaching the Gospel, administering the Sacraments, reproving the erring, visiting the sick, and comforting the afflicted, and is called the Power of Order. It is exercised by the Elders jointly, in Church courts, in the form of judgment or administration, and is called the Power of Jurisdiction."[25]

Specifically, who has the power to ordain? Preaching elders or all elders? In the end, Jesus Christ ordains, and it does not make a great deal of difference whether it be by the preaching presbyters, which is rather logical, or by both kinds of presbyters, which has the value of affirming that the whole church is behind that which is being done for and to the ordinand. If anything real happens to the ordinand, it is because Jesus Christ through his Spirit acts in and upon him. For such action the presbyters pray, and by the ancient custom of laying on of their hands symbolize their desire and make official declaration that in their judgment this man is fit to be a minister of the church universal. The key to all church power is in Jesus Christ. The danger of saying that it vests in all the people is that we make a fetish of democracy; worse, we open the way to such a low view of the ministry that when a minister preaches the whole counsel of God—and displeases us—we will fire him. The danger of saying that church power vests in the ministers is that if pushed too far it degenerates into a deadly clericalism. All Reformed thinkers seek to avoid both errors, but some on both sides of the issue have left themselves so unguarded in expressing their point of view that they imply more than they intend. It is only partially true to say that the church elects its ministers to be set apart from the generality of the common priesthood of believers; for God gave the ministry to the church. Church power may well inhere in the whole body, but it is exercised through its officers, whether jointly or severally. Church power is not given over to mob-ocracy. Some things cannot be decided by majority vote. In the Reformed tradition, chosen representatives govern a spiritual republic!—under Christ.

More ultimate than the question, Who holds the keys? or, Who has the power? is this: Is the power of the Holy Spirit moving mightily in the church of God and are his ministers faithfully serving him? For it is not by might nor by power (including hierarchical), but by my Spirit . . .

X

THE REFORMED MINISTER
AT WORK TODAY

Today the minister of Word and Sacrament has a tremendous task and a terrific responsibility. He is an ambassador of Jesus Christ to an age which is peculiarly insensitive to the deeper things of the Spirit— an age which halfway believes Nietzsche's "God is dead." He has to do many more things than his precedessors in office were expected to do. He has more creaturely comforts than most of them had, but he also works under greater pressure than did most of his predecessors. Men like Luther, Calvin, Baxter, and Wesley were able to do great things for God, under tremendous stress, but in general the pressure is probably greater today.

Scores if not hundreds of books have been published in recent years describing the work of the modern pastor. Some books take up specific aspects of the pastor's work, such as the pastor as counselor. Our purpose is to look at the minister's task in its totality.

There are various ways to describe the minister's work. The parish pastor is a jack of all trades, or a general practitioner. He has to be able to do many things and to do all of them at least fairly well. Precisely what is expected of the pastor of a particular church varies with the denomination and the region of the country. In general, the pastor is expected to carry out the traditional "offices" of the pastor. He is expected to be a *preacher*, and this is still his primary function in the eyes of most people, probably. He is to be a *pastor*, and this is coming to be his chief function in his own eyes. The pastoral office includes many subfunctions, such as pastoral counseling, pastoral calling, hospital visitation, ministry to sick and dying, and the conducting of funerals and weddings. All of these have been done in all ages by good pastors, though less self-consciously than today, and

sometimes on an inadequate theoretical basis. A parish pastor
is also a *priest*, in that he represents the people as he leads them in
public worship and in the sacraments. In their name he offers up sacrifices of praise and thanksgiving and prayers of petition, intercession,
and dedication. He is to be a *teacher*, and this in the dual sense of his
own teaching ministry and his leadership responsibility for the total
educational program of his congregation. He is to be an *organizer and
administrator*, and in this he needs to be faithful and efficient, but
herein he desperately needs to delegate responsibility and make use of
his laymen. He cannot, however, avoid being the counselor and adviser
to the many church organizations, even if he is wise enough to limit
the number of meetings of each he must attend. He is executive administrator of the program of the church. Further, the minister has the
responsibility of guiding his church in its relationships within the
community, and in active participation in interdenominational programs. He also takes part in the life and work of his own denomination. His ministry is not limited to his own local church, though it pays
his salary and deserves the major portion of his time and interest.
Historically, ministers have always had to do all of these things,
though the weight of emphasis has shifted from time to time. Today
the weight probably is no longer where it used to be—namely, on the
offices of preaching and pastoral work—but is on administration and
organization. Dr. Blizzard's careful study agrees with common obser-
vation on this point. No good parish pastor can avoid engaging in all
of these functions, though he will be better in some than in others.

Whether one starts with the traditional offices, or with the ancient
"prophet, priest, and king," there is no escaping the vast breadth of
the minister's task. His job is as varied as that of the medical general
practitioner, and as difficult. Just as most people most of the time do
not need medical specialists, so most people most of the time do not
need ecclesiastical specialists, but general practitioners, *pastors and
teachers*.

Today the pastoral minister has his task cut out for him. So much
in the modern era is in direct conflict with the deeper understanding of
the gospel. That many modern ministers spend more time in organization and administration than in study and sermon preparation is undeniable. Also undeniable is the appalling thinness of spiritual food

their parishioners sometimes receive. Many a pastor feels he is caught in the meshes of the organization and must spend his time keeping the wheels going around. Until pastor and people regain some understanding of who and what a minister is, this condition will continue. (The minister's office needs to become once more his study.)

A MAN OF GOD

In the Reformed tradition, the minister is first and foremost *a man of God*. This is his supreme obligation, to live so close to his Lord that he can reflect something of the Divine spirit in his own life and action. If a minister does not maintain the spiritual glow, if he does not spend adequate time in prayer and meditation and brooding study of the Bible, he cannot possibly be an adequate servant of the Word. He may be a good servant of the people at a superficial level, and dodge his responsibility to be a good servant of God. He may run a taxi service for the people of his congregation, participate in half a dozen community organizations, spend every week night in a meeting at the church, do janitor service regularly, and be a master of the mimeograph. The less perceptive members may think he is "a great guy" because he is so willing to do the work they ought to be doing, but the more thoughtful members will realize that their minister is so busy serving tables that he has ceased to serve God first. Unless the minister grows steadily in his own relationship to God, he will become in the end a pathetically shallow preacher and an inept pastor in times of deepest need.

The time has come for a revolution in the church. We must wake up to the driven state of many a modern minister, and help him regain his proper role as a man of God sent to be an ambassador of reconciliation, a servant of the Divine Word who serves the people most effectively as he serves the Word faithfully.

The people must cease to expect their pastor to do everything for them; the pastor must learn to put first things first. In any normal community, practically every church has a number of laymen who can serve on community boards and agencies as effectively as can the pastor. In most congregations, there are several adults who can carry on some of the routine and inescapable duties of organization and administration at least as well as can the pastor.

Denominational boards have established more and more departments, which in turn have set up programs which call for "committees in every congregation, presbytery and synod," to see that the work is well done. Denominational manuals are sometimes so detailed that they leave almost no place for creative imagination or initiative, and assume practically no intelligence on the part of the leaders who will use the manuals. Some of these programs are really necessary, but responsible executives need to recognize that they may be building a Frankenstein. Denominational general councils need to study with courage the numerous programs which the minister is supposed to "spark" in his local church, and ruthlessly cut out those which are not really essential.

In the United Presbyterian Church in the U.S.A., approximately 25 per cent of its active ministers are not in the pastorate, but are in some form of ministerial specialization, such as a teacher, missionary, board staff member, or a council of churches officer.[1] While undoubtedly many of these positions must be filled by ordained ministers, many of them could be handled by dedicated, well-trained laymen, to the end that some ministers could be released for pastoral work. While many of these positions are indispensable to current church work, some of them could be abolished to the good of the church. No particular individuals are to blame for the current situation; given our genius for organization, and the contemporary scene, it was almost inevitable. My thesis is that the church ought to wake up, rethink its mission, and endeavor to keep to an absolute minimum its use of ministers in non-pastoral posts in which laymen could serve effectively. In any case, the parish minister would do better work if the denominational programs were cut down to the essentials.

A PERPETUAL STUDENT?

The parish minister, the pastor-teacher, is "the man on the firing line." He has the most responsible position in the church. In many ways, "The pastor is the key." He really is . . . And we have created a situation in which he has neither the status nor the support that he needs. In recent years a disturbing trend has been observed in many seminaries. This has been the desire, not only of the top ten per cent of the students, but of many more who are just in the top forty per cent, to go on for a master's degree or even a doctorate, in the hope that eventually they will be called to teach in a college or seminary. The church will always need a handful of outstanding scholars to teach in theological seminaries and colleges. These men are the "Doctors" or teachers of Calvin and Knox, the men who keep the church's doctrine pure and vital and its leaders learned. Theirs is a significant task, and strategically their work is supremely important. Yet the church can use relatively few such persons. Seminary students as well as men in the pastorate need to realize that their richest contribution to the life of the church and the coming of the Kingdom probably will be as pastors of particular churches. The "Doctor" is as essential to the welfare of the church as is the parish bishop. However, the church needs far more local bishops than it does "Doctors." Every Reformed minister ought to be a student as long as he lives. He needs to be supremely at home in the Bible, but also truly interested in theology in its implications for life as men must live it. The wise pastor will always be studying some major theme, using the great, basic books, while he is doing his sermonic preparation also. The minister ought to be not only a first-rate Bible scholar, and a competent theologian who can communicate with people, but he also needs to be constantly alert to the political and sociological implications of his day. To preach an ancient gospel to a modern world, the minister must know Bible and theology, psychology and sociology, and how to relate all of these to the concrete existential situations of his people. Next to being a man of God, the modern minister ought to be a real student who will be able to speak to the condition of his people.

It is in connection with the Word of God that the pastor is a specialist. To unfold that Word to his people through sermon and teaching and life is his primary task. Any adult in the congregation can drive a car of juniors to day camp, but only the minister can exegete the eighth chapter of Romans or the forty-fifth of Isaiah. Many elders can make routine pastoral visits, but realistically only the pastor can carry out such functions as pastoral counseling to the grief-stricken, premarital counseling, and the deeper types of pastoral counseling.

Qualified laymen can and should carry much of the burden of administration and organization, which are in many aspects really functions
of the diaconate and the eldership and not of the pastor. The modern
pastor must be a capable organizer and a skillful administrator, but if
he is really skillful he will train his church officers to do much of this
work, or will put to work those already trained.

There are only so many hours in a day. If you do this, you cannot
do that. The minister needs to learn to discern the things that are more
excellent, *to learn his priorities*. And he needs to teach his people what
the priorities are. Sometimes wise elders can teach their pastors the
true priorities. The top priority of the minister is to be a man of God
—and this he cannot do unless he follows the example of his Lord and
goes apart awhile in prayer and meditation and study of the Word.

If the minister and his people recognize that he is a man called of
God—through his church—and set by God in this particular sphere
of responsibility, then they must give him *time* to be what God intends
him to be. He is called of God to be a man of God in a unique sense.
All Christians are called to be men of God, but the reason the minister
has no secular vocation is that he may spend full time in this specific
Christian service. The monk in his monastery, his life devoted to
prayer, is an extreme illustration of this uniqueness. All Christians are
to pray, but the minister is set apart from worldly cares and avoca-
tions in order that he may be a man of prayer. If he really understands
his priorities, he will spend much time in prayer. And he will be a
genuine student of the Bible, theology, and the modern scene. An ignorant minister cannot serve God's people well. Unless the minister
spends considerable time in prayer and in study he will learn the awful
judgment,

"The hungry sheep look up, and are not fed."[2]

City pastors have to fight, now, to maintain study habits. Some
wise and bold ones succeed, while a few keep up in part by virtue of
two months' vacations. The minister should train his people to understand that he MUST study if he is to be for them a true pastor who
can help them to grow in their life and mission. If the pastor does not
grow, he is not likely to equip his people for their ministry. It is essen-

tial for the pastor to keep three or four hours a day for study and meditation.

IN HIS OWN HOME

If the minister is a family man, then he is called by God to give some time to his own family. The bishop is to rule well over his own household, and this is impossible if he is never at home. Some time every week ought to be kept for his own family, including some evening meals. This time set apart for his own family should be flexible, but it should have a high priority. Too many ministers have been mediocre mates and poor fathers because they simply have not given the time to their own families that they should have given. Many ministers feel that if they reserve time for their own families they will neglect their people. If a church is really large enough to need a full-time minister, he will never get around to doing all the things that he thinks he ought to do. He should train his laymen to carry out their own ministry, and not do it for them. The compulsively driven minister who never has any time for his family ought to examine himself before God, and if that does not cause him to slow down, to be less pushed, and to find more time for his family, then he probably needs to consult a good pastoral counselor, or a psychiatrist!

A WORKER WITH PERSONS

The minister is a specialist in interpersonal relations. He has to work with people, and he should know about group dynamics. But his knowledge should never be used to manipulate people or to get them to do what he wants them to do. Rather, in love, he should endeavor to build up the people of God through the various structures and forms of church life, but always with emphasis not on structure *per se* but on the persons for whom the organization is developed. His interest in persons leads him to master basic principles of organization and administration and to develop laymen to carry on the necessary functions involved. (This should never be the chief work of a parish minister but may become a specialization of a few staff people.)

The primary task of the minister is to be a man of God, an ambassador of Christ, a steward of the mysteries of God, a representative of God to the people, and a pastor who loves and cares for these people because they are God's children. If he is this kind of man, then he cannot be just a cog in an organizational machine. He must be free to proclaim the Word of God as he understands it after he has agonized in study and in prayer to hear that word for his people. Imperfect, yes, that he surely will be, but to be treated lightly or disrespectfully, this never. As was his Lord, he is to be "prophet, priest, and king."[3]

THE CHURCH'S RESPONSIBILITY

These two things the church must do: (1) It must recognize that the church exists in order to be the medium through which Jesus Christ is continuing his ministry on the earth, and that every single Christian partakes of this ministry. (2) It must recognize that for the sake of order, God has set in his church ministers of Word and Sacrament, men called and ordained to special service in the church, that this set-apart ministry is worthy of respect, and that the word conveyed through the minister is to be "obeyed" insofar as that word is truly the Word of God.

Only through this kind of revolution can the church of today expect to find its more able sons and daughters hearing the call to the ordained ministry. When "every Christian is a minister," it is very easy for no Christian to take seriously the special responsibility of some Christians. When the ministry is composed of hired hands who must preach only what the people want to hear, no wise youth will desire to enter such a vocation. When ministers are caught in the wheels of administration, the rat race of the organization man, and are not allowed to accept and carry out their rightful priorities, no wonder they make little effort to recruit the finest youth of their congregation to the gospel ministry, and no wonder that the finest are likely to turn to science, or engineering, or medicine, or law, or business. All vocations need and deserve good men, but the gospel ministry deserves the best possible. Until the church recognizes its own doctrine of the ministry it cannot expect its finest sons and daughters to be ministers. God grant that the revolution may come soon. We need godly and able men, never on pedestals but always in the midst of their people, guiding them, living and learning with them, and ever sensitive for some sure word of God for our time. May the Holy Spirit call many of our finest to the ministry, and may Jesus Christ be Lord!

ECCLESIA REFORMATA, SEMPER REFORMANDA

One of the key concepts of the Reformation is that the true Reformed church is always being reformed. *Ecclesia reformata sed semper reformanda.* Applied to the ministry, this principle means that, while there will always be in the church as an organized institution the need for an ordained ministry, yet the precise forms of that ministry are flexible. History bears ample witness to that. Beyond question, as the future unfolds, there will be new understandings of the ministry, new duties, new priorities, while some of the old concepts, old duties, and old priorities will be recognized as outmoded. There already have been many changes, and there will be more. God did not give a static ministry to a static church, he gave a dynamic ministry to a church which is always on the move. The ordained ministry of Word and Sacrament is a permanent office, but the ministry is and must always be flexible and adaptable. Its forms will vary with changing circumstances and changing needs. Particular emphases will change from age to age and country to country, for the ministry is set in the church for the leadership of the church as it witnesses to God in its day and generation. The ministry which our Lord is carrying out in and through his church, in its life and community, is flexible and functional, designed to meet the basic needs of men in the existential situation in which they find themselves. The church as it witnesses in the world speaks to existing needs. The ordained minister now emphasizes pastoral work, now administration, now preaching, now teaching, now priesthood, as the need is most urgent.

But the clamorous needs of men tell but half the story. There is an ultimate. That ultimate is the nature of God as he is revealed in Jesus Christ. The ministry of Word and Sacrament is incorporated into that ultimate. "Rather, speaking the truth in love, we are to grow up in every way into him who is the head, into Christ, from whom the whole body, joined and knit together by every joint with which it is supplied, when each part is working properly, makes bodily growth and upbuilds itself in love" (Eph. 4:15-16). The immediate goals of the ministry are subject to the particular situation and the insistent pleas of men for help, but the ultimate goal is always the same, namely, "for the equipment of the saints . . . for the work of ministry, for building up the body of Christ, until we all attain to the unity of the faith and of the knowledge of the Son of God, to mature manhood, to the measure of the stature of the fulness of Christ . . ."(Eph. 4:12-13). This is the task of the church and this is the task of the ministers whom God calls, in every generation as long as the world lasts.

The minister, then, is called by God that he may "equip the saints for the work of ministry." (Note again that the comma is omitted after saints.) To lead God's people to carry out their ministry is always the function of the pastor. He also strives to build up the body of Christ, and this objective is not to be interpreted in narrow selfishness but in the spirit of John 3:16—the church is to be built up not for institutional glory but for the redemption of the whole world. There is a sense in which the body of Christ grows only as people are brought to know Jesus Christ as their Lord and Saviour—"until *we all* attain to the unity of the faith . . . to mature manhood." What clearer goal, what more challenging ultimate objectives, can one need? When the institutional church in visible form disappears in any given country or regional culture, the church God knows as his own will still be very much alive—even though its obvious forms or order have to be laid aside for a while. Were an atomic holocaust to wipe out all of our church buildings and millions of people, the forms of the ministry might change—at least for a while—but the ultimate functions would not change, for men would still need the Word of God mediated to their souls.

Appendix A

THE PASTORAL DIRECTOR

Richard Niebuhr, in his volume *The Purpose of the Church and Its Ministry*, suggested a concept of the ministry that has caught fire. The minister is the *pastoral director*. Niebuhr is correct in recognizing that the predecessor of the pastoral director is to be found in the pastoral bishop of an ancient church, such as Augustine, Bishop of Hippo, or the parish bishops of the Church of Scotland. "His first function is that of building or 'edifying' the church; he is concerned in everything that he does to bring into being a people of God who as a Church will serve the purpose of the Church in the local community and the world. [He carries on all the traditional offices of the minister, though from a new perspective.] . . . These and other less central activities of the ministry of all periods are carried on by the pastoral director, but the work that lays the greatest claim to his time and thought is the care of a church, the administration of a community that is directed toward the whole purpose of the Church, namely, the increase among men of the love of God and neighbor; for the Church is becoming the minister and its 'minister' is its servant, directing it in its service."[1]

There are great values in Niebuhr's approach. The church does have a mission to perform; Christ is continuing his ministry through the church. The minister of Word and Sacrament is inescapably the director of the church's program of life and ministry. Yet he is the *pastoral* director, not the big-operator type of minister. Administration does become his point of orientation in some cases, and in all cases it is a significant part of his task. This writer believes that already Niebuhr's thesis has been misconstrued to mean that the pri-

149

mary function of the minister is to be an organizer and administrator. The Blizzard studies showed that this is the way the modern minister is actually spending his time. And Niebuhr's treatment is not perfect. As long as the minister's workshop is called an office rather than a study, which Niebuhr accepts, so long is it likely that the big-operator concept may prevail and the people will be given lots of personality and powerful organization but little spiritual vitality and meatless sermons. The basic weakness of the Niebuhr thesis, which I accept as sound when the connotations of parish bishop accrue, is that he unwisely speaks of the minister as the servant of the church. Of course in one sense he is just that, but he is primarily the servant of the Lord, and he is responsible, at least in the Reformed tradition, not to his people but to his Lord for what he says and how he conducts his office. True, his brethren in presbytery have pastoral oversight of him, but he is not responsible to his session as to a board of directors, nor is he responsible to the congregation as to a group of stockholders. Niebuhr insists that "it is the Church, not he in the first place, that has a parish and responsibility for it."[2] That is only a half-truth. The church is set by God in this particular spot to minister the Word, but God has given this particular church this particular man to be its responsible leader, and the minister must guide the church in its gathering of the saints as well as in their edification. And guide he must in both areas. This is his ministry too! Just as there is a certain circularity in the relationship of the church and the Bible, so there is clear circularity in the relationship of the church and the minister. These are just other forms of the chicken-egg question!

Appendix B

THE RULING ELDER

Part of the genius of Presbyterianism is its concept of the ruling elder. The elder shares the rule with the pastor. He is a godly leader who gives time and talent and money and love to the work of the church. He is, and can well continue to be, that which makes Presbyterianism the envy of the churches on the right and on the left. Government by chosen representatives of the people, in the long run, is better than either autocracy (the Catholic churches) or pure democracy (the churches with congregational government). The eldership with its representative government is biblical as well as democratic, and constitutes a sound approach to church polity.

Thornwell and his followers were wrong in considering the ruling elder a presbyter in the full meaning of the biblical term. In the Old Testament, the elder was first literally an old man with presumed wisdom to guide and judge the people. It is highly probable that in the time of Christ and the apostolic church, this literal sense of the word continued, but it was soon, if not always, supplemented by a deeper note. Not only was the elder, presumably, mature in years and in judgment, he was also to be a man of noble character and "apt to teach." It is likely, but not certain, that the elders ordained by Paul and Barnabas were not ministers in a full-time sense, but laymen who gave part-time but devoted leadership to the church. If a church was governed by elders, they carried out their work in a council—our session. Almost inevitably, one man came to take pre-eminence in the council, perhaps as the permanent moderator. In time, the permanent moderator came to be the pastor, the overseer, though his pastorhood was shared by all the elders, or, better, presbyters. This one presbyter eventually came to be called *the* bishop, but he still had his session of elders—who at the beginning were equated with bishops. It is highly probable that the session in the early church was literally composed of elders-presbyters-bishops—all one and the same—but with one man soon taking permanent leadership. The elder worthy of double honor was the prototype of our modern pastor, who both rules and teaches. The other elders were basically laymen in our modern sense, but laymen who gave a great deal of time to the church leadership. From around A.D. 200 to the present, the word "presbyter" was attached to the priest in the Roman Church, and in Protestantism it became attached to the minister. Presbyters are ministers. The ruling elder came into his own again with Presbyterianism, but he came in as a lay officer of the church, not as a ministerial officer. The ruling elder in the United States of America in the 1960's is not a minister except in the very general sense that all Christians are ministers and in the particular sense that church officers are ministers. He is a layman, chosen to represent the laity in the government of the church. He supremely represents the people, and when the effort is made to call him a minister, or a presbyter in the post-apostolic sense, his usefulness is perverted. The glory of Presbyterianism is that laymen genuinely share in the government of the church as representatives of the people.

A traditional Presbyterian phrase is "the parity of presbyters." When we say parity of elders, instead of parity of presbyters, we mean that both ministers and lay elders are ruling elders, that both possess the right to govern the people. But we mean, further, that in the courts of the church the ruling elder has equal vote. He judges every issue, he participates in every vote, along with the preaching elders. He is eligible for any office the church court can give, including the moderatorship. But there are limits, both legal and realistic. The legal limits are that the ruling elder in most Presbyterian churches has to be given permission by presbytery to preach, and he cannot administer the sacraments or marry people under any circumstances. The realistic limits are that the preaching elder supposedly attends every meeting of presbytery, whereas the ruling elder may attend only occasionally. Because of greater familiarity with procedure, and far greater training and theological education, and sometimes better facility of tongue, the preaching elder normally has a distinct advantage over the ruling elder. There are certain ruling elders who regularly attend presbytery and who themselves are so able that from any standpoint they are the equal of any preaching elders present. The rank and file of ruling elders, however, do feel themselves at some disadvantage in the church courts above the session. In the local church session, of course, the elders are strongly in the majority; in the higher courts there is theoretical equality of numbers and in presbytery there may be a majority of elders. There is no reasonable ground for ruling elders to feel resentful because the ministers usually know their way around better in church courts. This is inevitable. The only way it could be changed would be to abolish the ordained ministry, and to allow no men to receive special training or to give full time vocationally to the ministry. Unless absolute democracy is our god, this is nonsense. The ideal of any Presbyterian court is teamwork, not competition between ruling elders and pastors. A few men try to drive a wedge between clergy and laity, but generally there is a wonderful relationship, with genuine sharing of responsibility. In the session the minister rightly exercises leadership, but he does not dominate. The whole session governs the people.

Appendix C

PRESBYTERIANS AND APOSTOLIC SUCCESSION

American Presbyterians seldom if ever have had to face the question of apostolic succession, but if the Consultation on Union proposals are seriously considered, this question will be involved. In the British Isles this issue has always been of great importance, for the two major countries in the United Kingdom have two different state churches: England the Episcopal; Scotland the Presbyterian. From the sixteenth century there has been heated discussion as to the validity of orders. The high church Episcopalians have insisted that the Episcopal Church has a pure order of ministry, for its ministers have been properly ordained by bishops who were ordained by bishops—on back to the beginning, to the apostles. The Pope half a century ago flatly stated that Anglican orders are invalid, that they are not in the true apostolic succession. Presbyterians in Scotland, living so close to the Church of England, and having in their own land a small but spiritually significant Episcopal Church, and having centuries of complex relationships, have always had to stand up and affirm stalwartly the validity of Presbyterian orders. The Scottish Presbyterians have defended themselves along several lines.

1. Many scholars correctly say that lineal descent from the apostles by the hands of succeeding bishops is utterly impossible to prove.

2. Having made this assertion, they go on to add that literal succession is not necessary, but that succession to the doctrine of the apostles is a note of the true church and of a genuine, valid ministry.

3. Some make the point, as did the Pope, that the English orders, in a literal sense, have grave weaknesses.

154

4. All point out that the Church of England at the beginning of the English Reformation gladly recognized the validity of the Continental Reformers, and there were instances of recognition of Scottish orders.

5. George Gillespie insists that the thing that matters is not a literal lineal succession but the perpetuity of both ministry and church in Christian faith and life. "If our believing the holy church universal, and that in all ages Christ hath had and shall have a true church, doth not infer that we must believe the church either always visible, or always pure, so our believing a perpetual ministry doth not infer that therefore we must believe either a lineal or visible succession of ministers, or their purity and preservation from error."[1] This viewpoint, that God has preserved and will preserve his church and the ministry, and that its value depends not upon laying on of hands by bishops but on the vitality of its faith and the obedience of its life to the Lordship of Christ, is probably the position most Presbyterians would take today.

6. Some Scottish Presbyterians have been sufficiently impressed by the Anglican claims to make a counterclaim—that Presbyterians, too, have apostolic succession. Lord Balfour of Burleigh, for instance, wrote: "It is undoubtedly true that the first generation of Reformed preachers had been nearly all Roman presbyters; that within a few years they began to ordain new presbyters by the laying on of hands; and that there is therefore in the Scottish Presbyterian Churches a *perpetua successio presbyterorum* from before the Reformation."[2] Few Reformed leaders have pressed this point. However, when tilting lances with the Anglicans, it has seemed to some Reformed thinkers to be worthwhile to be able to make this assertion about validity. The English Presbyterians boldly proclaim a lineal descent, "And they alone who have received it [church power] from the Apostles can derive and transmit it to other Ministers."[3] They also said, ". . . our Ministry is descended to us from Christ *through* the Apostate Church of *Rome*, but not *from* the Apostate Church of *Rome*."[4] Sprott, Witherspoon, *et al.*, also insist that Presbyterians can claim apostolic succession at least as validly as can Rome or Canterbury. And probably this is true.

7. Some Scots believe that for decency and order ministers should be ordained by the hands of preaching presbyters whose ordination

is valid and in the succession, but that in special circumstances God
can and does fill the gap. ". . . nor doe we hold a constant ordination
of Pastors in a continuall line of succession from the Apostles made
by Pastors; the succession may be interrupted, but then God himself
supplyeth the want of ordinary ordination appointed by himself."[5]

In summary, Presbyterians believe that their ministry is apostolical in that it is called and commissioned by God through duly appointed officers for the apostolical mission; that their claim to lineal
succession is perfectly good but that this fact is not important, for
what matters is loyalty to apostolic faith and living obedience to the
Head of the church, and the profound assurance that it is Christ who
has given *this* ministry to the church, received and validated by her
call and ordination.

Notes and Acknowledgments

I. THE MINISTER TODAY

1. Samuel W. Blizzard, "The Minister's Dilemma," *The Christian Century*, Vol. LXXIII (April 25, 1956). Professor Blizzard's careful sociological study of American ministers has significant implications. When this material is published in book form, it will be indispensable for a study of the actual practices of the minister.
2. Bruce Reinhart, *The Institutional Nature of Adult Christian Education* (Philadelphia: The Westminster Press, 1962), especially Ch. II. See also Martin E. Marty, *The New Shape of American Religion* (New York: Harper & Brothers, 1959) ; Gibson Winter, *The Suburban Captivity of the Churches* (Garden City, N. Y.: Doubleday & Company, Inc., 1961).
3. Nelson N. Foote and Leonard S. Cottrell, Jr., *Identity and Interpersonal Competence* (Chicago: University of Chicago Press, 1955).

II. THE BIBLICAL VIEW OF THE MINISTRY

1. Daniel Jenkins, *The Gift of Ministry* (London: Faber and Faber, 1947), p. 20.
2. Brooke Foss Westcott, *The Gospel According to St. John*, Vol. II (Grand Rapids: Wm. B. Eerdmans Publishing Company, 1950), p. 146.
3. J. K. S. Reid, *The Biblical Doctrine of the Ministry* (Edinburgh: Oliver and Boyd Ltd., 1955), p. 1.
4. T. W. Manson, *The Church's Ministry* (Philadelphia: The Westminster Press, 1948), p. 107.
5. Ephesians 1:22-23; 2:19-22; 4:11-16; 5:21-33; John 15:1-11.
6. Manson, *op. cit.*, p. 107.
7. T. F. Torrance, *Royal Priesthood* (Edinburgh: Oliver and Boyd Ltd., 1955), p. 35.
8. *The Westminster Confession of Faith*, XXVII.3; *The Book of Church Order*, Presbyterian Church in the U.S. (1961 edition), p. 20. Scottish writers often assume this concept.
9. Reid, *op. cit.*, pp. 1-17.
10. Oliver Chase Quick, *Doctrines of the Creed* (New York: Charles

Scribner's Sons, 1938), p. 327. Cf. Alan Richardson (note 13 below), p. 319.

11. Gregory Dix, "The Ministry in the Early Church c.A.D. 90-410," Kenneth E. Kirk, ed., *The Apostolic Ministry* (London: Hodder & Stoughton Ltd., 1946), pp. vi, 228-232.

12. Manson, *op. cit.*, "The Apostolate," pp. 34-56.

13. Alan Richardson, *An Introduction to the Theology of the New Testament* (New York: Harper & Brothers, 1959), p. 315.

14. *Ibid.*, p. 322.

15. John Calvin, *Institutes of the Christian Religion*, edited by John T. McNeill, translated by Ford Lewis Battles (Philadelphia: The Westminster Press, 1960), Vol. 2., IV. iii. 6 (p. 1059).

16. See also 2 Thessalonians 3:14; Philemon 21; Romans 1:5; as well as 3 John 9 and especially Hebrews 13:17, "Obey your leaders and submit to them; for they are keeping watch over your souls, as men who will have to give account."

17. Manson, *op. cit.*, p. 107.

18. See John Knox, "Romans, Exegesis," in *The Interpreter's Bible*, Vol. IX (Nashville: Abingdon Press, 1954), p. 586. The translations of J. B. Phillips, R. F. Weymouth, James Moffatt, Edgar Goodspeed, and the New English Bible all have here the idea of rule.

19. Anders Nygren, *Commentary on Romans*, translated by Carl C. Rasmussen (Philadelphia: Muhlenberg Press, 1949), pp. 422-423.

20. John Calvin, *Commentary on the Epistles of Paul the Apostle to the Corinthians*, tr. by John Pringle (Grand Rapids: Wm. B. Eerdmans Publishing Company, 1948), p. 398.

21. *Ibid.*, p. 404.

22. Clarence Tucker Craig, "First Corinthians, Exegesis," in *The Interpreter's Bible*, Vol. X (Nashville: Abingdon Press, 1953), p. 162.

23. Calvin, *First Corinthians, op. cit.*, p. 413.

24. Alfred Plummer and Archibald Robertson, *First Epistle of St. Paul to the Corinthians, The International Critical Commentary* (Edinburgh: T. & T. Clark, 1894), p. 278.

25. Clarence Craig, *op. cit.*, p. 163.

26. *Ibid.*, p. 164.

27. F. W. Beare, "Ephesians, Exegesis," in *The Interpreter's Bible*, Vol. X (Nashville: Abingdon Press, 1953), pp. 690-691.

28. See G. Stoeckhardt, *Commentary on St. Paul's Letter to the Ephesians*, translated by Martin S. Sommer (St. Louis: Concordia Publishing House, 1952), p. 200; William Owen Carver, *The Glory of God in the Christian Calling* (Nashville: The Broadman Press, 1949), p. 150.

29. Charles Hodge, *A Commentary on the Epistle to the Ephesians* (New York: Robert Carter and Bros., 1856), pp. 226-227.

30. J. Armitage Robinson, *St. Paul's Epistle to the Ephesians* (London: Macmillan and Company, Ltd., 2nd ed., 1904), p. 181.

31. G. Stoeckhardt, *op. cit.*, p. 200.

III. THE BIBLICAL WORDS: ELDER, BISHOP, DEACON

1. Rudolph Bultmann, *A Theology of the New Testament*, Vol. II, translated by Kendrick Grobel (London: SCM Press Ltd., 1955), pp. 111-118.
2. Martin Rist, "Revelation, Exegesis," in *The Interpreter's Bible*, Vol. XII (Nashville: Abingdon Press, 1957), pp. 402, 410; cf. Evelyn Underhill, *Worship* (New York: Harper & Brothers, Torchbook Edition, 1957), pp. 91-92; Allen Cabaniss, "A Note on the Liturgy of the Apocalypse," *Interpretation*, Vol. VII, No. 1 (January, 1953), pp. 78-86.
3. See Clement of Rome, "The Letter of the Church of Rome to the Church of Corinth, Commonly Called Clement's First Letter," translated by Cyril C. Richardson, *Early Christian Fathers* (Philadelphia: The Westminster Press, 1953); also, the *Didache* may well be as early as A.D. 130.
4. J. B. Lightfoot, *Saint Paul's Epistle to the Philippians* (London: Macmillan and Co., Ltd., 4th revised edition, 1900), Dissertation on "The Christian Ministry," pp. 181-269; see also pp. 95-99. In essential agreement with Bishop Lightfoot are Alan Richardson, *op. cit.*, p. 325; Rudolph Bultmann, *op. cit.*, p. 102; Floyd V. Filson, *Jesus Christ the Risen Lord* (Nashville: Abingdon Press, 1956), p. 208.
5. John Knox, "The Ministry in the Primitive Church," in *The Ministry in Historical Perspectives*, edited by H. Richard Niebuhr and Daniel D. Williams (New York: Harper & Brothers, 1956), p. 21. Used by permission of Harper & Row, Publishers, Incorporated.
6. Clement of Rome, *op. cit.*, *circa* A.D. 96.
7. 1 Timothy 3:1-7; 5:17-19; Titus 1:5-9; *Didache*.
8. Eduard Schweitzer, *Church Order in the New Testament*, translated from the German by Frank Clarke (London: SCM Press Ltd., 1961), p. 49; G.H.C. Macgregor, "The Acts of the Apostles, Exegesis," in *The Interpreter's Bible*, Vol. IX (Nashville: Abingdon Press, 1954), p. 90, agrees with Chrysostom that probably the Seven were "neither presbyters nor deacons," but held a unique office parallel to that of the Twelve; Alan Richardson (*op. cit.*, p. 330) says, "There is certainly here no hint of an 'order' of deacons—a word which is not found in Acts"; Rudolph Bultmann (*op. cit.*, Vol. I, p. 56) says the Seven were not deacons but representatives of the Hellenistic party, while H. J. Carpenter, "Minister," in Alan Richardson, ed., *A Theological Word Book of the Bible* (New York: The Macmillan Company, 1950), p. 149a, thinks it difficult to co-ordinate the office of the Seven with any of the later forms. *Per contra*, Ph. H. Menoud, "Ministry," in J.-J. Von Allmen, ed., *A Companion to the Bible* (New York: Oxford University Press, 1958), p. 263b, "Without doubt the author of the Acts regards the Seven as the forerunners of the deacons, who are not mentioned in Acts . . ."
9. John Knox, *op. cit.*, p. 21.
10. J. Armitage Robinson, *op. cit.*, pp. 97, 181.
11. Clement of Rome, *op. cit.*, 44, lines 1-4 (pp. 63-64).
12. *Ibid.*, Introduction, pp. 38-39. Richardson notes: "The deposition of

the local Corinthian rulers leads him to set forth a hierarchical view of the ministry and to stress the need of submission to the duly elected clergy" (p. 38).

13. K. J. Woollcombe, "The Ministry and the Order of the Church in the Works of the Fathers," in *The Historic Episcopate*, edited by Kenneth M. Carey (London: Dacre Press, 1954), p. 46. Woollcombe continues: "It was quite a sufficient guarantee of the continuance of an orderly ministry, that only men whose work for Christ had been manifestly blessed by the Spirit should succeed to the episcopate, with the consent of the whole church."

14. Burnett Hillman Streeter, *The Primitive Church* (New York: The Macmillan Company, 1929), pp. ix, 268.

15. Ignatius, Bishop of Antioch, "Epistle to the Smyrnaeans," *circa* A.D. 112, Henry Bettenson, ed., *Documents of the Christian Church* (New York: Oxford University Press, 1947), p. 89.

16. Cyprian, Bishop of Carthage, 248-258, "De Catholicae Ecclesiae Unitate," Ep. LXVI.7 in Bettenson, *op. cit.*, p. 104.

17. Philip Schaff, *History of the Christian Church*, Vol. II, *Ante-Nicene Christianity* (Grand Rapids: Wm. B. Eerdmans Publishing Company, 5th ed., 1950), p. 158.

18. While there is little doubt that the Apostle Peter went to Rome, there is also little doubt that the Roman church has drawn false conclusions about Peter. Matthew 16:18 needs to be balanced by 18:18-20. Peter was a natural and forceful leader, but Jesus' words should not be taken to mean that Peter was to be "the permanent, official, authoritative head of the entire church," from whom by lineal apostolic succession would come the popes. For a fair, brief treatment see Floyd V. Filson, *op. cit.*, pp. 203-205; for a comprehensive treatment see Oscar Cullmann, *Peter: Disciple, Apostle, Martyr*, translated from the German by Floyd V. Filson (Philadelphia: The Westminster Press, 1953; revised 1962).

19. For an excellent treatment of the unfortunate growth of celibacy, based on a twisted view of sex, see Derrick S. Bailey, *Sexual Relation in Christian Thought* (New York: Harper & Brothers, 1959). For good but shorter treatments see William Graham Cole, *Sex in Christianity and Psychoanalysis* (New York: Oxford University Press, 1955), and Roland H. Bainton, *What Christianity Says About Sex, Love, and Marriage* (New York: Association Press, 1957).

20. Roland H. Bainton, "The Ministry in the Middle Ages," in Niebuhr and Williams, *op. cit.*, pp. 84ff.

21. George H. Williams, "The Ministry in the Later Patristic Period," in Niebuhr and Williams, *op. cit.*, p. 68.

22. Gregory the Great, *Pastoral Care*, *circa* A.D. 600 (Westminster, Md.: The Newman Press, 1950).

IV. THE EARLY CONTINENTAL REFORMERS ON THE MINISTRY

1. Martin Luther, quoted by Wilhelm Pauck, "The Ministry in the Time of the Continental Reformation," in Niebuhr and Williams, *op. cit.*, p. 112.

2. See Martin Luther, "Address to the German Nobility," quoted in James L. Ainslie, *The Doctrines of Ministerial Order in the Reformed Churches of the 16th and 17th Centuries* (Edinburgh: T. & T. Clark, 1940), p. 5.
3. John T. McNeill, *A History of the Cure of Souls* (New York: Harper & Brothers, 1951), p. 190.
4. Pauck, *op. cit.*, pp. 112-113.
5. Martin Luther, *Letters of Spiritual Counsel*, edited and translated by Theodore G. Tappert (Philadelphia: The Westminster Press, 1955), p. 304.
6. *Ibid.*, p. 299.
7. *Ibid.*, p. 313.
8. Luther, quoted in Pauck, *op. cit.*, p. 115.
9. From *Calvin: Institutes of the Christian Religion*, edited by John T. McNeill, translated by Ford Lewis Battles. Vol. 2, IV.iii.1 (p. 1053). Copyright © 1960, W. L. Jenkins. The Westminster Press. Used by permission.
10. *Ibid.*, IV.iii.1 (p. 1053).
11. *Ibid.*, IV.iii.1 (p. 1054).
12. *Ibid.*, IV.iii.2 (p. 1055).
13. *Ibid.*, IV.iii.4 (p. 1057).
14. *Ibid.*, IV.iii.5,6 (pp. 1058-1059).
15. *Ibid.*, IV.iii.7 (p. 1059).
16. *Ibid.*, IV.iii.7 (p. 1060).
17. *Ibid.*, IV.iii.8,9 (pp. 1060-1061).
18. *Ibid.*, IV.iii.10 (p. 1062).
19. *Ibid.*, IV.iii.11 (pp. 1062-1063).
20. *Ibid.*, IV.iii.11 (p. 1063).
21. *Ibid.*, IV.iii.15 (pp. 1065-1066).
22. *Ibid.*, IV.iii.15 (p. 1066).
23. *Ibid.*, IV.iii.16 (pp. 1066-1068).
24. A. Dakin, *Calvinism* (Philadelphia: The Westminster Press, 1946), p. 122.
25. Wilhelm Niesel, *The Theology of Calvin*, translated by Harold Knight (Philadelphia: The Westminster Press, 1956), p. 203.
26. John Calvin, *Theological Treatises*, translated and edited by J.K.S. Reid (Philadelphia: The Westminster Press, 1954), p. 58.
27. John T. McNeill, *The History and Character of Calvinism* (New York: Oxford University Press, 1954), p. 161.
28. Calvin, *Theological Treatises, op. cit.*, p. 63.
29. W. Pauck, *op. cit.*, p. 130.
30. Huldreich Zwingli, quoted and translated by Ainslie, *op. cit.*, p. 7.
31. Heinrich Bullinger, "On the Holy Catholic Church," in *Zwingli and Bullinger*, edited by G. W. Bromiley (Philadelphia: The Westminster Press, 1953), pp. 321, 322, 324.
32. Quoted in Ainslie, *op. cit.*, pp. 7-8.
33. *Ibid.*, p. 8.
34. *Ibid.*, p. 9. Compare Philip Schaff, *The Creeds of Christendom*, Vol. III (New York: Harper & Brothers, 1877), p. 374.

V. IN THE BRITISH ISLES

1. G. W. Sprott, ed., *Scottish Liturgies of the Reign of James VI* (Edinburgh: William Blackwood and Sons, 1901), p. x.
2. William Dunlop, ed., *A Collection of Confessions of Faith . . . of Publick Authority in the Church of Scotland* (Edinburgh: James Watson, Printer, Vol. II, 1722), p. 383.
3. *Ibid.*, p. 405.
4. *Ibid.*, pp. 408, 409.
5. *Ibid.*, p. 409.
6. *Ibid.*, p. 411.
7. *Ibid.*, pp. 411-412.
8. *Ibid.*, p. 412.
9. *Ibid.*, p. 416.
10. *Ibid.* (*The First Book of Discipline*), pp. 523-524.
11. *Ibid.*, p. 525.
12. *Ibid.*, p. 526.
13. *Ibid.*, p. 526.
14. *Ibid.*, p. 528.
15. *Ibid.*, pp. 528-529.
16. *Ibid.*, p. 529.
17. Professor Hugh Watt, New College, University of Edinburgh, class lecture, 1956.
18. Dunlop, *op. cit.* (*The First Book of Discipline*), p. 529.
19. *Ibid.*, p. 530.
20. Martin Luther, *Works*, Vol. 11, pp. 9-10.
21. Dunlop, *op. cit.* (*The Second Buik of Discipline*), p. 760.
22. *Ibid.*, p. 762.
23. *Ibid.*, p. 764.
24. *Ibid.*, p. 765. Some old manuscripts show *Servandis* in place of Middis.
25. *Ibid.*, pp. 770-771.
26. *Ibid.*, p. 771.
27. *Ibid.*, p. 772.
28. The London Provincial Assembly of 1654, *Jus Divinum Ministerii Evangelici* or *The Divine Right of the Gospel Ministry* (2 parts in 1 volume, printed for G. Latham, *et al.*, 1654), Vol. I, p. 1. (This volume is hereafter referred to as JDME.)
29. JDME, Vol. I, p. 4.
30. George Gillespie, *CXI Propositions Concerning the Ministerie and Government of the Church* (Edinburgh: Evan Tyler, 1647).
31. *Acts of the General Assembly of the Church of Scotland, 1638-1842*, Reprinted from the original edition under the supervision of the Church Law Society (Edinburgh Printing Co., 1843), p. 71.
32. *Ibid.*, p. 137.
33. JDME, Vol. II, p. 99.
34. JDME, Vol. I, p. 76.
35. JDME, Vol. I, p. 80.
36. Quoted in James Walker, *The Theology and Theologians of Scotland*,

Chiefly of the 17th and 18th Centuries (Edinburgh: T. & T. Clark, 2nd edition, revised 1888), p. 191.

37. Quoted in *ibid.*, p. 192.
38. George Gillespie, *A Treatise of Miscellany Questions*, Ch. III, p. 15, in *The Presbyterian's Armoury*, Vol. II (Edinburgh: Robert Ogle and Oliver and Boyd, 1844).
39. JDME, Vol. I, pp. 138f.
40. Thomas F. Torrance, *Conflict and Agreement in the Church*, Vol. 2, *The Ministry and the Sacraments of the Gospel* (London: Lutterworth Press, 1960), pp. 49-50.
41. In this section I derived help from Norman Sykes, *The English Religious Tradition* (London: SCM Press Ltd., 1953).
42. Thomas Leishman, ed., *The Westminster Directory* (Edinburgh: William Blackwood and Sons, 1901), p. 195.
43. *Ibid.*, pp. 195, 196.
44. *Ibid.*, p. 196.
45. *Ibid.*, pp. 204-205.
46. *Ibid.*, p. 203.
47. *Ibid.*, p. 197.
48. *Ibid.*, p. 198.
49. *Ibid.*, p. 197.
50. Dunlop, *op. cit.*, Vol. I., *The Westminster Confession of Faith* (1719), pp. 151, 152.
51. Dunlop, Vol. I, *Larger Catechism*, Answer 158, p. 345.
52. *Ibid.*, Answer 159, pp. 345, 346.
53. Leishman, *op. cit.*, p. 17.
54. *Ibid.*, p. 91.
55. *Ibid.*, p. 37.
56. *Ibid.*, pp. 60-61.
57. Richard Baxter, *The Reformed Pastor*, edited by Hugh Martin (London: SCM Press Ltd., 1956), p. 9.
58. Baxter, *ibid.* (quotation from his *Autobiography*), p. 10.
59. *Ibid.*, p. 73.
60. *Ibid.*, p. 74.
61. *Ibid.*, p. 22.

VI. CHANGING CONCEPTS OF THE MINISTRY IN AMERICA

1. William Warren Sweet, *Religion in Colonial America* (New York: Charles Scribner's Sons, 1942), p. 87.
2. Quoted in *ibid.*, p. 204.
3. *Ibid.*, p. 292.
4. From *The Forming of an American Tradition* by Leonard J. Trinterud, p. 142. Copyright 1949, W. L. Jenkins. The Westminster Press. Used by permission.
5. *Ibid.*, pp. 159ff.
6. Quoted in Trinterud, *ibid.*, p. 269.
7. Quoted, *ibid.*
8. W. W. Sweet, *Religion on the American Frontier, 1783-1840*, Vol. II: *The Presbyterians* (New York: Harper & Brothers, 1936), pp. 65-66.

9. Ralph C. Deal, "The Present-Day Requirements of the Ministry," *The Union Seminary Magazine*, Vol. XVII (1905-06), p. 138. Cf. Matthew Van Lear, "The Power of the Ministry Purely Personal, Never Official," *The Union Seminary Magazine*, Vol. V (1893-94), p. 193.

10. Sweet, *Religion in Colonial America*, pp. 231-232.

11. Trinterud, *op. cit.*, p. 62.

12. *Ibid.*, pp. 201-202.

13. Quoted in Trinterud, p. 202.

14. Quoted, *ibid.*, p. 266.

15. Sweet, *Religion in Colonial America*, p. 289.

16. *Ibid.*, p. 292.

17. Trinterud, *op. cit.*, p. 201.

18. *Ibid.*, pp. 204-205.

19. Donald G. Tewksbury's standard work is unavailable to me. See Sweet, *Frontier*, Vol. II, pp. 75-76.

20. *Ibid.*, p. 82.

21. These quotations from the *Minutes of Transylvania Presbytery, 1786-1837*, may be found in Sweet, *Religion on the American Frontier*, Vol. II: *The Presbyterians*, pp. 131, 134, 135, 139, 141, 146, 160, 162, 188-189. A manuscript copy of these minutes is in the library of the Louisville Presbyterian Theological Seminary. See pages 2, 3, 7, 19-20, 47, 50, 88, 131-132, 139, 250-251.

22. Excerpts from the *Minutes of Cumberland Presbytery*, in Sweet, *Frontier*, Vol. II, p. 285.

23. James Henley Thornwell, *Collected Writings*, Vol. IV, *Ecclesiastical*, edited by John B. Adger and John L. Girardeau (Richmond: Presbyterian Committee of Publication, 1873), "The Gospel Ministry," p. 568.

VII. WHO IS A MINISTER?

1. From *Agents of Reconciliation* by Arnold B. Come, pp. 99, 118, 119. Copyright © 1960, W. L. Jenkins. The Westminster Press. Used by permission.

2. *The Westminster Confession of Faith*, XXVII.iii.

3. Source not now available.

4. Charles Hodge, *What Is Presbyterianism?* An Address Delivered Before the Presbyterian Historical Society, May 1, 1855 (Philadelphia: Presbyterian Board of Publication, 1855), pp. 38-39.

5. John Mason, "The Church of God," XI "Officers," *The Christian's Magazine*, Vol. III (May, 1810), p. 269.

6. Quoted in J. E. Lesslie Newbigin, *The Reunion of the Church* (London: SCM Press, 1948), p. 148.

7. Charles Hodge ("Theophilus"), "Is the Church of Rome a Part of the Visible Church?" *The Princeton Review*, Vol. 18 (1846), p. 331.

8. Scottish Church Society, occasional papers IV, *Presbyterian Orders* (Edinburgh: A. Eliot, 1926), pp. 6, 7.

9. *Acts of the General Assembly of the Church of Scotland, op. cit.*

10. J. B. Lightfoot, *op. cit.*, p. 268.

11. Donald MacLeod, *The Doctrine and Validity of the Ministry and Sacraments of the National Church of Scotland* (Edinburgh: William Blackwood and Sons, 1903), pp. 177-178.
12. T. W. Manson, *Ministry and Priesthood: Christ's and Ours* (Richmond: John Knox Press, 1959), pp. 70-71.
13. John Calvin, *Commentaries on the Epistles of Paul to the Galatians and Ephesians,* tr. from the Latin by William Prings (Wm. B. Eerdmans Publishing Company, 1948), p. 282 (on Eph. 4:12).
14. Thomas R. English, "The Pastor in His Pulpit," *The Union Seminary Magazine,* Vol. XIV (1902-03), p. 85.
15. *The Union Seminary Review,* Vol. XXXV (January, 1924), pp. 145, 149, 150, 153.
16. Henry Sloane Coffin, *Communion Through Preaching; The Monstrance of the Gospel* (New York: Charles Scribner's Sons, 1952), pp. 12 and 9.
17. R. M. Patterson, "The Supply of Ministers," *The Presbyterian Review,* Vol. I (July, 1880), p. 541.
18. Anonymous, "Plain Truth . . ." (Glasgow: Robert Sanders, Printer, 1693), pp. 5-6.
19. *Ibid.,* pp. 8-9.
20. *Ibid.,* p. 14.
21. *Ibid.,* p. 10.
22. *Ibid.,* pp. 17-18.
23. William Wishart. A sermon preached to the General Assembly, May 6, 1725, by William Wishart, Principal of New College.
24. The Synod of Missouri, Presbyterian Church, U.S., in 127th Annual Session, June 22-24, 1959.
25. Wishart, *op. cit.,* pp. 39, 40.
26. *The Biblical Repertory and Theological Review,* Vol. VIII (July, 1836), p. 380.
27. *The Minutes of the General Assembly of the Presbyterian Church,* 1844, Vol. X, p. 357.
28. *The Princeton Theological Review,* Vol. XIV (January, 1916), pp. 83, 86, 89, 91.
29. "Relations of our Theological Seminaries to our System of Church Government," *The Presbyterial Critic and Monthly Review,* edited by Stuart Robinson & Thomas E. Peck, Vol. I (January, 1855), pp. 7-13.
30. "The Church of God: XV, Officers &c," *The Christian's Magazine,* Vol. III (October, 1810), p. 568.

VIII. BECOMING A MINISTER

1. Thomas R. English, "A Call to the Ministry," *Union Seminary Magazine,* Vol. VII (1895-96), p. 103.
2. John Calvin, *Institutes,* IV.iii.11 (Vol. II, p. 1063).
3. JDME, Vol. I, p. 126.
4. "What Constitutes a Call to the Gospel Ministry?" *The Biblical Repertory and Presbyterian Review,* Vol. III, New Series (1831), pp. 207-208.
5. Thomas Cary Johnson, "The Call to Office in the Church Established

by the Apostles," *The Union Seminary Magazine*, Vol. VI (1894-95), pp. 248-249.

6. Robert L. Dabney, "What Is a Call to the Ministry?" in *Discussions*, Vol. II, *Evangelical*, ed. by C. R. Vaughan (Richmond: Presbyterian Committee of Publication, 1891).

7. "A Call to the Ministry of the Gospel," *The Literary and Evangelical Magazine*, Vol. 9 (1826), pp. 113-117.

8. This is the thesis of Rev. James O. Speed, Jr., Director, Department of Enlistment, Presbyterian Church, U.S. Robert Clyde Johnson agrees. "The body, not the individual, is charged with responsibility to discern the gifts and provide the Church with an ordained ministry." "The Christian Ministry" in Robert Clyde Johnson, ed., *The Church and Its Changing Ministry* (Philadelphia: Office of the General Assembly, U.P.U.S.A., 1961), pp. 34-35.

9. Particularly relevant: *The Book of Church Order of the Presbyterian Church in the United States*, 1961 edition, ch. 24, "Candidates for the Ministry of the Word" (pp. 61-65), and ch. 27, "The Ordination and Installation of Ministers" (pp. 71-73). See also *The Constitution of the United Presbyterian Church in the United States of America*, Form of Government (1962-63 edition), Chapters XVIII, "Of Candidates for the Gospel Ministry" (pp. 140-142), XIX, "Of the Ordination of Ministers" (pp. 143-146), and XX, "Of the Calling and Installation of Ministers" (pp. 147-151a); and see *The Constitution of The Reformed Church in America* (1961 edition), article 3, "Licensure and Ordination," pp. 8-12.

10. *The Book of Church Order of the Presbyterian Church in the United States*, Form of Government § 27-4 (p. 72); *Constitution*, Reformed Church, 112:5, 11c, 12.

11. Form of Government (U.P.U.S.A.), XIX.6 (p. 145), (1962-63 ed.).

12. *Book of Church Order* (U.S.), Form of Government § 27-2 (pp. 71-72).

13. *Ibid.*, § 27-5.

14. Form of Government (U.P.U.S.A.), *op. cit.*, XIX.2 (p. 143).

15. Form of Government (U.S.), § 27-5; Form of Government (U.P.U.S.A.), XIX.2 (p. 143).

16. JDME, Vol. I, pp. 133-134.

17. *Ibid.*, pp. 134-135.

18. *Ibid.*, p.135.

19. *Ibid.*, p. 137.

20. *Ibid.*, pp. 138-139.

21. Samuel Rutherford, *A Peaceable and Temperate Plea*, p. 263, quoted in JDME, Vol. I, p. 140.

22. JDME, Vol. I, p. 139.

23. *Ibid.*, Vol. I, p. 144.

24. "May a Minister Demit the Ministerial Office?" *The Presbyterian Quarterly Review*, Vol. V (1856-57), p. 102.

25. T. C. Johnson, *op. cit.*, p. 260.

26. JDME, Vol. I, p. 168.

27. United Church of Canada, Draft of a Statement Concerning Ordina-

tion to the Ministry (Executive Committee of the General Council, 1926), p. 54.

28. George Hill, *Lectures in Divinity*, 2nd ed., 1825, edited by Alex. Hill (New York: Robert Carter), p. 697.

29. James Bannerman, *The Church of Christ: A Treatise on the Nature, Powers, Ordinances, Discipline, and Government of the Christian Church*, Vol. I (Edinburgh: T. & T. Clark, 1868), pp. 469-470.

30. Lesslie Newbigin, *op. cit.*, p. 161, including a quotation from the Scheme of Union of the Church of South India, p. 7.

31. George W. Sprott, *The Worship and Offices of the Church of Scotland* (Edinburgh: William Blackwood and Sons, 1882), p. 212.

32. A. Come, *op. cit.*, pp. 116, 117-118.

33. For a different view of *the* minister's place, see Wesner Fallaw, *Church Education for Tomorrow* (Philadelphia: The Westminster Press, 1960), pp. 13-23, and J. Stanley Glen, *The Recovery of the Teaching Ministry* (Philadelphia: The Westminster Press, 1960), pp. 9-26.

34. *The Book of Common Worship* (Philadelphia: Board of Christian Education—edition for the Presbyterian Church in the U.S., 1946), "Form and Order for the Ordination to the Holy Ministry," pp. 229-230.

35. Newbigin, *op. cit.*, pp. 162-163.

36. M. Bernoulli, "Laying on of Hands," in *A Companion to the Bible*, ed. by J.-J. Von Allmen (New York: Oxford University Press, 1958; © Lutterworth Press), pp. 230-231.

37. JDME, Vol. I, pp. 182, 183.

38. *Minutes of the General Assembly, Presbyterian Church in the U.S.A.*, Vol. X, 1842-1844 (1843, p. 183; 1844, pp. 370, 393).

39. *Ibid.*, p. 370. For a powerful protest and its answer, see pp. 390-394 of the Minutes of the 1844 Assembly. "Your committee would suggest that the act of induction is ministerial, not judicial. And as, in respect to baptism, the elders jointly with the pastor determine who shall be admitted to this ordinance, yet the pastor only administers it; so in ordination, the whole Presbytery determine the fitness of the candidate, but only the ministers present induct into office. This, we believe, has been the universal practice under this rule." *Minutes of the General Assembly, Presbyterian Church in the U.S.A.*, 1859-1869, inclusive. *New School Branch*, Vol. II (Philadelphia: The Stated Clerk of the General Assembly, 1894), pp. 68-69.

IX. THE REFORMED MINISTER: PLACE AND POWERS

1. John Calvin, *Commentaries on the Catholic Epistles* (Wm. B. Eerdmans Publishing Company, 1948), pp. 143-144.

2. Quoted in Ainslie, *op.cit.*, p. 97, translated by Ainslie.

3. Quoted in Ainslie, p. 98.

4. D. Calderwood, *A History of the Kirk of Scotland*, IV, 209-217, quoted in Ainslie, *op. cit.*, p. 99.

5. Dunlop, *op. cit.*, Vol. II, p. 766.

6. Ainslie, *op. cit.*, pp. 105-120.
7. *Book of Church Order*, § § 10-1, 10-2, 10-3, 10-4; Form of Government (U.P.U.S.A.), Ch. VIII, especially Par. 2.
8. *Book of Common Worship*, pp. 229-230.
9. John Calvin, *Tracts and Treatises*, Vol. III, tr. by Henry Beveridge, edited by Thomas F. Torrance (Grand Rapids: Wm. B. Eerdmans Publishing Company, 1958), p. 357.
10. Dunlop, *op. cit.*, Vol. II, pp. 84-85.
11. *Ibid.*, p. 246.
12. Ainslie, *op. cit.*, p. 66.
13. G. W. Sprott, ed., *The Book of Common Order of the Church of Scotland, Commonly Known as John Knox's Liturgy* (Edinburgh: William Blackwood and Sons, 1901), p. 34.
14. John Calvin, *Letters*, ed. by Jules Bonnet, Vol. III, tr. by M. R. Gilchrist (Philadelphia: Presbyterian Board of Publication, 1858), p. 67. Letter CCCLXII to Gaspar Liser, Geneva, August 27, 1554.
15. JDME, Vol. I, p. 76.
16. Dunlop, *op. cit.*, Vol. II, p. 771.
17. James D. Smart, *The Teaching Ministry of the Church* (Philadelphia: The Westminster Press, 1954), pp. 77, 79. See pp. 68-83, especially pp. 79-80.
18. Fallaw, *op. cit.*
19. *The Due Right of Presbyteries* (London, 1644), p. 137.
20. Quoted by G. D. Henderson (source lost).
21. Hill, *Lectures in Divinity*, *op. cit.*, p. 698.
22. Charles Hodge, "The Church of England and Presbyterian Orders," in *The Princeton Review*, 1854, pp. 377ff.; see also Hodge, *Church Polity*, p. 142.
23. Charles Hodge, *What Is Presbyterianism?* (Philadelphia: Presbyterian Board of Publication, 1855), pp. 41-42, 40.
24. *Book of Church Order* (1961), pp. 19-20.
25. *Ibid.*, Ch. I, § § 1-1, 1-2, 1-3, 1-4 (p. 22).

X. THE REFORMED MINISTER AT WORK TODAY

1. Frederick C. Maier, "The Ministry Today," in Robert Clyde Johnson, *op. cit.*, p. 166. In 1960, of living ministers in the United Presbyterian Church in the U.S.A., 60.1 per cent were in the pastoral ministry; 6.2 per cent were missionaries or chaplains; 5.1 per cent were board executives and secretaries; 5.2 per cent were teachers or other educators; 2.5 were students, evangelists, in transit, or listed as miscellaneous; and 13.8 per cent were retired. Alarming is the fact that 7.1 per cent were undesignated. But for two centuries the church in America has been worried over the loss of ordained men to the undesignated (presumably secular) category.
2. John Milton, *Lycidas*, line 125.
3. *The Westminster Larger Catechism* (Richmond: John Knox Press, revised edition, eleventh printing 1961), Answer 42.

APPENDIX A

1. H. Richard Niebuhr, *The Purpose of the Church and Its Ministry* (New York: Harper & Row, Publishers, 1956), pp. 82-83.
2. *Ibid.*, p. 91.

APPENDIX C

1. George Gillespie, *A Treatise of Miscellany Questions*, 1649 (Ch. I, p. 3), in *The Presbyterian's Armoury*, Vol. II (Edinburgh: Robert Ogle and Boyd and Oliver, 1844).
2. Lord Balfour of Burleigh, *Presbyterianism in Scotland*, p. 44, quoted in James Moffatt, *The Presbyterian Churches* (New York: Doubleday, Doran & Co., Inc., 1928), p. 120.
3. JDME, Vol. I, p. 186.
4. *Ibid.*, Vol. II, p. 33.
5. Samuel Rutherford, *A Peaceable and Temperate Plea*, p. 261, quoted in Alexander Martin, *Presbyterian Orders and Admission of Ministers from Other Churches: A Memorandum* (Edinburgh: Church of Scotland Committee on Publications, 1941), p. 30.

A Select Bibliography

This bibliography does not include the commentaries consulted, nor the Minutes of the General Assemblies. Omitted also are books with a chapter or so on church and ministry, as well as the vast multitude of books on the practical work of the minister. Books marked * are particularly significant, while those marked ** are significant but not readily accessible.

BOOKS

** *Acts of the General Assembly of the Church of Scotland, 1638-1842* (Edinburgh: Edinburgh Printing and Publishing Co., 1843. Church Law Society Edition).

* Ainslie, James L., *The Doctrines of Ministerial Order in the Reformed Churches of the 16th and 17th Centuries* (Edinburgh: T. & T. Clark, 1940).

Baillie, Robert, *The Letters and Journals of Robert Baillie*, 1637-1662, edited by David Laing (Edinburgh: Bannatyne Club Edition, 1841).

Bannerman, James, *The Church of Christ: A Treatise on the Nature, Powers, Ordinances, Discipline, and Government of the Christian Church*, Vol. I, edited by his son (Edinburgh: T. & T. Clark, 1868).

Baxter, Richard, *The Reformed Pastor*, edited by Hugh Martin (Richmond: John Knox Press, 1963).

Bettenson, Henry (ed.), *Documents of the Christian Church* (New York: Oxford University Press, 1947).

* Bromiley, G. W., *Christian Ministry* (Grand Rapids: Wm. B. Eerdmans Publishing Co., 1959).

Bultmann, Rudolf, *A Theology of the New Testament*, Vol. II, tr. by Harold Knight (London: SCM Press, 1955).

* Calvin, John, *Commentaries*, tr. and ed. by Joseph Haroutunian (Philadelphia: The Westminster Press, 1958).

* Calvin, John, *Institutes of the Christian Religion*, 2 vols., ed. by John T. McNeill, tr. by Ford Lewis Battles (Philadelphia: The Westminster Press, 1960).

* Carey, Kenneth M. (ed.), *The Historic Episcopate* (London: Dacre Press, 1954).

* Come, Arnold B., *Agents of Reconciliation* (Philadelphia: The Westminster Press, 1960).

Dakin, A., *Calvinism* (Philadelphia: The Westminster Press, 1946).

** Dunlop, William (ed.), *A Collection of Confessions of Faith . . . of Publick Authority in the Church of Scotland,* 2 vols. (Edinburgh: James Watson, Printer, 1719, 1722).

Ehrhardt, Arnold, *The Apostolic Succession in the First Two Centuries of the Church* (London: Lutterworth Press, 1953).

** Gillespie, George, *CXI Propositions Concerning the Ministerie and Government of the Church* (Edinburgh: Evan Tyler, 1647).

Gregory the Great, *Pastoral Care* (Westminster, Md.: The Newman Press, 1950).

* Hanson, Anthony T., *The Pioneer Ministry* (Philadelphia: The Westminster Press, 1961).

Harnack, Adolf, *The Constitution & Law of the Church in the First Two Centuries* (New York: G. P. Putnam's Sons, 1910).

* Henderson, G. D., *Church and Ministry: A Study in Scottish Experience* (London: Hodder and Stoughton, 1951).

* Henderson, G. D., *The Claims of the Church of Scotland* (London: Hodder and Stoughton, 1957).

* Henderson, Robert W., *The Teaching Office in the Reformed Tradition* (Philadelphia: The Westminster Press, 1962).

Hort, F. J. A., *The Christian Ecclesia* (New York: The Macmillan Company, 1898).

* Jalland, T. G., *The Origin and Evolution of the Christian Church* (London: Hutchinson, 1950).

* Jenkins, Daniel, *The Gift of Ministry* (London: Faber and Faber, 1947).

* Jenkins, Daniel, *The Protestant Ministry* (Garden City, N.Y.: Doubleday & Co., Inc., 1958).

* Johnson, Robert Clyde (ed.), *The Church and Its Changing Ministry* (Philadelphia: Office of the General Assembly, United Presbyterian Church in the U.S.A., 1961).

** *Jus Divinum Ministerii Evangelici,* by members of the London Provincial Assembly (London: G. Latham, *et al.,* 1654).

* Kirk, Kenneth E. (ed.), *The Apostolic Ministry* (London: Hodder and Stoughton Ltd., 1946).

* Kraemer, Hendrick, *A Theology of the Laity* (Philadelphia: The Westminster Press, 1959).

** Leishman, Thomas (ed.), *The Westminster Directory* (Edinburgh: William Blackwood and Sons, 1901).

* Lindsay, Thomas M., *The Church and the Ministry in the Early Centuries* (London: Hodder and Stoughton, 1902).

Lowrie, Walter, *Ministers of Christ* (Louisville: Cloister Press, 1946).

* Luther, Martin, *Letters of Spiritual Counsel,* ed. and tr. by Theodore G. Tappert (Philadelphia: The Westminster Press, 1955).

MacGregor, Geddes, *Corpus Christi: The Nature of the Church*

According to the Reformed Tradition (Philadelphia: The Westminster Press, 1959).

** MacLeod, Donald, *The Doctrine and Validity of the Ministry and Sacraments of the National Church of Scotland* (Edinburgh: William Blackwood and Sons, 1903).

McNeill, John T., *A History of the Cure of Souls* (New York: Harper & Brothers, 1951).

Macpherson, John, *The Doctrine of the Church in Scottish Theology* (Edinburgh: MacNiven & Wallace, 1903).

* Manson, T. W., *The Church's Ministry* (Philadelphia: The Westminster Press, 1948).

* Manson, T. W., *Ministry and Priesthood: Christ's and Ours* (Richmond: John Knox Press, 1959).

** Martin, Alexander, *Presbyterian Orders and Admission of Ministers from Other Churches: A Memorandum* (Edinburgh: Church of Scotland Committee on Publications, 1941).

* Newbigin, J. E. Lesslie, *The Reunion of the Church* (London: SCM Press, 1948).

* Niebuhr, H. Richard, *The Purpose of the Church and Its Ministry* (New York: Harper & Row, Publishers, 1956).

* Niebuhr, H. Richard, & Williams, Daniel D. (eds.), *The Ministry in Historical Perspectives* (New York: Harper & Brothers, 1956).

Niebuhr, H. Richard, Williams, Daniel D., & Gustafson, James M., *The Advancement of Theological Education* (New York: Harper & Brothers, 1957).

Niesel, Wilhelm, *The Theology of John Calvin* (Philadelphia: The Westminster Press, 1956).

* Pittinger, W. Norman, *The Church, the Ministry, and Reunion* (Greenwich, Conn.: Seabury Press, Inc., 1957).

** *Plain Truth: A Seasonable Discourse of the Duties of People to Their Pastors* (Glasgow: Robert Sanders, Printer, 1693; reprinted 1713).

Quick, Oliver Chase, *Doctrines of the Creed* (New York: Charles Scribner's Sons, 1938).

* Reid, J.K.S., *The Biblical Doctrine of the Ministry* (Edinburgh: Oliver and Boyd Ltd., 1955).

* Richardson, Alan, *An Introduction to the Theology of the New Testament* (New York: Harper & Brothers, 1959).

Robinson, Wm. Childs, *Columbia Theological Seminary and the Southern Presbyterian Church, 1831-1931* (Decatur, Ga.: Dennis Lindsey Printing Company, Inc., 1931).

Scottish Church Society, *Presbyterian Orders* (Edinburgh: A. Eliot, 1926).

* Smart, James D., *The Rebirth of Ministry* (Philadelphia: The Westminster Press, 1960).

* Smith, Elwyn A., *The Presbyterian Ministry in American Culture, A Study in Changing Concepts, 1700-1900* (Philadelphia: The Westminster Press, 1962). This book came too late to be used. It seems to be able and provocative.

** Sprott, George W., *The Worship and Offices of the Church of Scotland* (Edinburgh: William Blackwood and Sons, 1882).

* Story, Robert H., *The Apostolic Ministry in the Scottish Church* (Edinburgh: William Blackwood and Sons, 1897).

Streeter, Burnett Hillman, *The Primitive Church* (New York: The Macmillan Company, 1929).

* Sweet, William Warren, *Religion in Colonial America* (New York: Charles Scribner's Sons, 1942).

* Sweet, William Warren, *Religion on the American Frontier, 1783-1840,* Vol. II: *The Presbyterians* (New York: Harper & Brothers, 1936).

Sykes, Norman, *Old Priest and New Presbyter* (New York: Cambridge University Press, 1956).

Sykes, Norman, *The English Religious Tradition* (London: SCM Press Ltd., 1953).

The Pulpit Guarded, by a Friend to Truth and Peace (Edinburgh, abridged edition, 1748).

Thornwell, James Henley, *Collected Writings,* 4 vols., edited by John B. Adger and John L. Girardeau (Richmond: Presbyterian Committee of Publication, 1873).

* Torrance, Thomas F., *Conflict and Agreement in the Church,* Vol. 2, *The Ministry and the Sacraments of the Gospel* (London: Lutterworth Press, 1960).

* Torrance, Thomas F., *Royal Priesthood* (Edinburgh: Oliver and Boyd Ltd., 1955).

* Trinterud, Leonard J., *The Forming of an American Tradition* (Philadelphia: The Westminster Press, 1949).

Walker, James, *The Theology and Theologians of the Church of Scotland, Chiefly of the 17th and 18th Centuries* (Edinburgh: T. & T. Clark, 2nd edition, revised 1888).

* Wotherspoon, H. J., & Kirkpatrick, J. M., *A Manual of Church Doctrine According to the Church of Scotland,* revised and enlarged by T. F. Torrance and Ronald Selby Wright (London: Oxford University Press, 1960).

MAGAZINES

In addition to the *Scottish Journal of Theology* and current American theological journals, the author read relevant articles and reviews in a number of religious periodicals written by advocates of the Reformed tradition during the nineteenth century. The list includes:

The Biblical Repertory and the Princeton Review (also called later the *Princeton Quarterly and Princeton Review*). In four series, 1825-1884 (Charles Hodge, editor, 1825-1871). Imprint varies.

The Christian's Magazine, 1806-1811. New York, John Mason, editor.

The Literary and Evangelical Magazine, 1818-1828. Title varies. Richmond, John Holt Rice, editor.

The Presbyterial Critic, January, 1855—September, 1856. Baltimore.

The Presbyterian Magazine, 1851-1860. Philadelphia, C. Van Rensselaer, editor.

The Presbyterian Quarterly, 1887-1904. Richmond, G. B. Strickler, *et al.*, editors.

The Presbyterian Quarterly Review, 1852-1862. New York and Philadelphia, B. J. Wallace, editor.

The Presbyterian and Reformed Review, 1890-1902. New York, B. B. Warfield, *et al.*, editors.

The Princeton Theological Review, 1903-1929. Imprint varies. Edited by the faculty.

The Southern Presbyterian Review, 1847-1885. Columbia, S. C.

The Spirit of the Nineteenth Century, 1842-1843. Baltimore, R. J. Breckinridge, editor.

The Union Seminary Magazine, superseded by *The Union Seminary Review*, 1889-1946. Richmond. Edited by various faculty members.

Index